The ANONYMOUS DISCIPLE

GERARD E. GOGGINS

Ambassador Books, Inc.
Worcester, Massachusetts

ISBN 1-929039-02-6
Library of Congress Catalog Card Number 99-65094

Published in 1999 in the United States by Ambassador Books, Inc.
71 Elm Street, Worcester, Massachusetts 01609
(800) 577-0909

Printed in Canada.

The Anonymous Disciple was originally published in hard cover (ISBN 0-9646439-9-5) by Assumption Communications in 1995.

For current information about all titles from Ambassador Books, visit our website at: www.ambassadorbooks.com

Dedication

In gratitude to two good soldiers, tried and true,
and to their special friend.

Prologue

That night, when he walked in, was the first time I took a really good look at him. He was bone thin and hunched over — he must have been in pain — but his smile was so broad, so all-encompassing, that one would never have suspected it. He was dressed in black, but the knees and elbows of his suit were shiny with age, and his Roman collar had yellowed and was ringed with a faint line of perspiration where it came in contact with his neck. He had a long white cigarette between the long thin fingers of his left hand, and with his right hand he used a cane for support. As he looked for a seat he seemed very ancient and shopworn.

He was tall. Even when he was hunched over, as he invariably was, he stood about six feet, but he was wafer thin and very fragile. He looked as if he had endured a thousand harrowing experiences stretched over ages, and hidden in the lines around his eyes were the echoes of the pain he had lived with for half a century. But what really defined him was his smile — huge, radiant, unquestioning. When he smiled at you, he seemed absolutely delighted to be in your presence, as if he had waited all day for that moment.

Once he sat down they flocked to him, especially the women. And he, in turn, welcomed them with that big grin. As he spoke, he occasionally spilled drops of coffee on his trousers, and as he wiped them away, a long ash would fall from his cigarette. He brushed the ashes off, without paying much attention, as if they were a kind of inside joke, and as he brushed, he ground most of the ashes into his creaseless, shiny black trousers.

I sat a few seats away from him, watching skeptically. What was going on here, I wondered? Were those people who came up to him giving or getting? Were they comforting or being comforted? One by one they came, holding their cups of coffee, and sitting down in those ubiquitous folding chairs they have at bingo games and Alcoholics Anonymous meetings. They exchanged a few words. They laughed. At first, I thought that perhaps they were humoring his senility. But there was joy there. And it was coming from him. He was like a gas station attendant giving a full tank to each person who pulled up at the pump. But he was pumping them up with joy. Strange man. Jesuits were supposed to be larger than life. They were supposed to be strong, soldierly, and proud. But he was frail and humble. Indeed, he was tattered. What had happened to his pride? What had happened to his tailor?

In a way, I had hoped that he really was senile. I don't mean that I wanted him to be any more afflicted than he was. It was just that his smile offended me. If it was real, and not the product of a doddering mind wrapped in the mists of senile memories, then in a way it was my accuser. The smile rebuked despair. It rebuked fear and anxiety and sorrow. It said, "All is well." It said, "There is joy. There is peace. There is love."

I got up to get myself a cup of coffee, and by the time the meeting started, I had forgotten about the old priest. I had other things to think about. I was filled with a titanic anxiety. It roared through me like a wild animal. It screamed as it caromed around my skull. My heart raced and my hands trembled, but I sat without moving, without letting on to those around me the awful war that was being waged within me. Fear. Fear of suddenly becoming a maniac, of standing up and screaming, of running from the hall raving — having crossed the line into insanity, where one is forever lost amidst the horrors and distortions, the shadows and the pain.

I had a difficult time paying attention once the meeting started. I was what they called "jiggy." I had heard them talk of having a head like a can of worms. And I thought of the inside of my skull — all those ideas squirming around, squeezing against each other, not being able to tell one idea from another, or the beginning of an idea from the end. It is hard to listen when one sick strand of thought wraps itself around another and another and another and they all become convoluted and knotted. Greasy thoughts. Worms.

I wanted to leave, but I was afraid to. I was afraid to stay, too. But I stayed. Straining to hear a word. Straining to get just one thought to take home with me. Something that could ease the chaos within me. I crossed my legs and uncrossed them. I fumbled with a cigarette. I wanted to light it, and I didn't. I wanted to stop smoking, and I did not. "Can't we take a break?" I wondered. "Can't we all get up and stretch our legs and go to the bathroom?"

And then he got up, and the applause was raucous. It was like Babe Ruth in Yankee Stadium. A few people actually shouted. He smiled as he hobbled toward the microphone. He even waved. I tried to concentrate, but at first

I only got snatches of what he said. He talked about uppers and downers, about taking downers to get up and uppers to get down. He talked about being catatonic and about losing his love for music and literature and sports. He struck a nerve. I feared going catatonic, of becoming a latter-day Silas Marner. And I had lost music and literature and sports. I began to concentrate, and I forgot the worms burrowing around my skull.

He looked out over the audience and his smile was beatific. "I know it's hard," he said. His voice was tender and full of sympathy. "Especially at first. When we have so much fear and we feel so badly. 'Poor Father Jim,' I used to tell myself, 'Oh, poor Father Jim. How did a nice guy like you wind up in a place like this?' " He smiled and his audience roared. He sniffed sheepishly. "Oh, shed a tear for poor Father Jim," he said. And again they laughed, most of them.

"And when I wasn't filled with that awful self-pity, there were the fears and the anxieties and all those thoughts, and my fellow priests looking at me and wondering when I was going to fall this time. All these terrible feelings. And nothing to take them away. No pills. No booze. You know. You know how hard it is. You can't trust and you can't believe. You just have to hang on. You have to keep coming to halls like this and listening to people like me. People who have gone before you, who have suffered what you are suffering, and who have come out of it."

I was touched by his understanding and by his compassion, and I found myself hanging on his words, as if he had begun to fill an inner hunger. And then, apropos of nothing, almost as if it were an aside, he said something that changed my life — a sentence that pinioned me, a sentence — that in that large hall with all those people — I believed was directed at me alone. His words cut through my inner turmoil. They cut through to the very heart of my being. They surrounded and defined me, and they were the beginning of the great revelation of my life.

I had told no one of my inner chaos, but this senile-looking priest seemed to understand it. And perhaps, as impossible as it seemed, he had a solution for it. I looked around the hall. No one was looking at me. They were all intent on what he was saying. They were laughing, and some of them were nodding their heads in agreement.

I don't remember the end of the meeting, and I hardly remember leaving. And when I did, I paid no attention to the large crowd of people who clustered in the driveway in front of the Congregational Church where the meeting was held or to the faint wail of a siren in the distance. I was obsessed by that one sentence. I kept repeating it to myself. I pondered it. I examined it. I digested it. And when I doubted it, I pictured Father Jim, hunched over the microphone, smiling, talking, laughing. He was so frail. But he was so certain.

That night marked the beginning of my great interior adventure. I have thought of it many times since. Years later, the image of smiling frailty still remained with me, and I wondered what road he had taken to get to the point where his words intersected with my pain. This man, who had seemed hardly more than a scarecrow, had so impressed me and had been so instrumental in changing my life that I decided, finally, to trace his history, to find out how it was that on the pivotal night of my life, he happened to be there in his shiny black suit and stained yellow collar.

Part One

Echoes

Chapter One

For the past week the hard edge of winter had been blunted. It was not a spring thaw, but at least it was a reminder that winter, even in New England, does not last forever. The temperatures had been in the forties during the day and had hovered around twenty at night. There had been some snow, an inch one day, a couple the next, even four inches on Tuesday, but in Worcester that was considered hardly a dusting, barely enough to call out the plows and sanders, but enough to emphasize the bleakness of the season and the drabness of the city.

It was dusk now, the most sorrowful part of the day, as the taxicab wound through the square at the foot of Vernon Street, and even if the cold was muted, it was still winter, grey was still the dominant color, and the city was still dirty.

Fred stared out the window. The wind was stirring little clouds of dust in the gutter. This morning after Mass, the sun had been shining, and Fred had felt the hope of spring. He had felt that life was about to return, not only to the earth, but also to himself. But now he was again seized by melancholy as he was each day that he took a cab to the hospital. And each day, the melancholy deepened, and each day the ride became more grim.

The cab stopped for a traffic light in front of a bar which people in the land-locked city called the Yacht Club. It was a dingy-looking place where a man could get lost for a week or a month, maybe a lifetime. A tall thin man in a disheveled black overcoat crossed in front of the cab. A brown paper bag, the badge of the wino, was sticking out of his coat pocket. He walked on his heels, not fast, not slow, to the inner cadence that every wino seems to hear. There was no rush or expectancy to the man. He moved with a vacant determination as if he was being carried along by something more powerful than himself, some derelict spirit that propelled him through the square and toward the bar's doors. The driver put the cab in first gear and started up the hill toward the hospital. The drunk was behind them. He would play out his little drama of trying to gain admittance to the Yacht Club before an empty street corner.

The hospital lobby was crowded, the atmosphere almost festive. Fred walked past the front desk and up a couple of stairs to the elevators.

"He looks like a movie star," a young blonde woman in a student nurse's uniform said.

"Yeah, but that's not enough," her companion said. She, too, was a student nurse, but she was heavier and not as attractive. "My dad says the country isn't ready for a Catholic president."

The first student nurse seemed disappointed. "What do you think about Kennedy, Father?" she asked.

Fred looked quite blank. He had never gotten used to the way perfect strangers felt free to drag priests into private conversations, and he was not expecting to be drawn into this one.

"You know, Father," she persisted, "Jack Kennedy. Do you think he can be president?"

The blank look left his eyes as he focused his gaze on her, but the expression on his face betrayed his lack of interest. "I don't know," he said.

The elevator doors opened and the three of them got on. The plain-looking student nurse pushed the number three button and turned to the priest. "Where to, Father?"

Very slightly, almost imperceptibly, Fred's head started to wag from side to side. It was exasperating, but there was nothing he could do about it. He had learned long ago that the more he tried to control it, the more it would shake.

"Six," he said. The psychiatric unit was on the sixth floor and the two students were immediately interested.

"That must be interesting work up there," the plain student said.

"She'd like to be a psychiatric nurse, Father," the blonde said. She hesitated for a split second. "You're not the chaplain are you, Father?"

They both knew that she knew he was not the chaplain. His head shook a little more perceptibly. "No. I'm from Holy Cross. I teach."

"Oh. Are you visiting a friend?" the plain one asked.

He was put off by their persistence or maybe embarrassed by it. Whatever the feeling, his head suddenly stopped wagging.

The elevator hitched slightly and slowed. "Yes, it's a friend of mine."

"Oh, it must be the Jesuit who's up there. Father, uh, Father what's-his-name."

The elevator doors opened but no one moved.

"This must be your floor," Fred said.

"What is his name, Father?" she persisted.

He surrendered. "Father Collins."

"That's right," she replied. "Father Jim Collins. I took care of him when he was sick last year. He's such a nice man. It's too bad."

The two young women got off the elevator and broke in different directions. "See you afta," the blonde called to her friend.

— ✧ —

Things were more professional on the sixth floor. Mother Mary Joseph was sitting at the desk going over the charts. Her presence was a comfort to Fred. Had it not been for her, the hospital would not have accepted Jim as a patient. The last time he had been released, Jim had been told he could not come back. But when Fred found Jim half dead on the floor of his room, he had called the nun and she arranged for Jim to be admitted to another floor. Once he started to recover physically, he was moved to the psychiatric unit.

She looked up from her paper work. "Hi, Father Fred." Her smile was warm.

"Hi, Sister. How is he tonight?"

She shrugged. "He'll be all right," she said in a matter-of-fact tone.

"Well, I'll go in and see him if I may."

"Sure, Father. Go right ahead."

James David Collins, S.J. sat on the side of his bed staring toward the window. If he was aware that someone had entered the room, he gave no sign of it. He looked old and emaciated. His fine features were too fine, too sharp, and the smile that was always with him was gone. He sat on the edge of the bed as if in a daze. His eyes were open but unfocused. A bright white T-shirt showed at the neck of his pale blue pajamas. It accented his fragile jaw and his jutting Adam's apple. His navy blue bathrobe hung in folds around his torso. He seemed lost in it, shrunken and very remote.

"Hello, Jim," Fred said.

There was silence. Not even a look.

Fred took a pack of Chesterfield regulars out of his pocket.

"Want a cigarette, Jim?"

There was no answer. Fred took off his black raincoat and draped it over the back of a chair. He sat down with his back to the window examining his friend. It was the fact that Jim would not take a cigarette that distressed him most. Jim was a heavy smoker, and he loved Chesterfields. But now he was too depressed or preoccupied to even glance at the package. Perhaps it was more than preoccupation or depression, Fred thought. Perhaps his mind was gone. Perhaps it was never coming back.

The routine had gone on for more than a month. Fred would come to the hospital and try to engage Jim in conversation. Jim seemed unable to acknowledge his presence. After fifteen or twenty minutes of trying to make even the smallest of small talk, Fred would lapse into silence. After an hour or so, the visit would end.

After the first week, Fred had gone to Mother Mary Joseph.

"He doesn't seem to know me. Do you think my coming here does any good?"

"It helps," she assured him. "Keep coming. One of these days he'll snap out of it."

So Fred came to the hospital each evening. But it was very difficult for him. The light had gone out of Jim. There was no spark. Jim would sit on the side of the bed, feet dangling, shoulders hunched, his vacant eyes gazing toward the blackness outside the window. It was painful for Fred to look at this shell of a man. Jim was only forty-nine, but he looked seventy. He looked like an old man who should be locked away in an old priest's home.

The two of them had been an unlikely pair of friends. Jim was outgoing and full of fun. He was the one who would arrange the picnics or get a group together to go to the race track. He loved to travel and lecture. He was exuberant by nature. Fred was quite the opposite. He was quiet, intro-spective, a scholar, a theologian. "Penseroso," Jim called him. Perhaps because they were fellow sufferers or perhaps because each had something the other lacked, they had become friends. "Pals, great pals," Jim would say.

Alcohol had been brutal to them both. Its effects were just more obvious in Jim. In January, after Jim had failed to come to the dining room for the second day in a row, Fred had gone in search of him. He had found his friend sprawled on the floor, unconscious. Jim was like a crumpled page that someone had tossed in a corner. He weighed less than ninety pounds. Fred lifted him up, with the effort it would take to pick up a pile of laundry, and laid him on the bed. Then he had called Mother Mary Joseph.

It was the booze. Jim had taken a lot of pills, too, but it was the booze that had brought him back to the hospital. It had been whittling him down for years. And in the end, he had been unable to carry on, to teach, or to take part in the life of the community. He could not even make it to dinner. He was ravaged. All he could do was drink. Night after night. Day after day. A derelict priest in a house full of Jesuits. An outcast.

In the end, everyone gives up on a drunk. The kindest, most charitable, most well-meaning people become exasperated. They try to help, and it comes to nothing. They become frustrated, but they try again. And again. And finally they turn their backs. They were silently relieved when Jim did not come to the dining room. They were spared seeing him shake or watching him make a scene with a kitchen worker. No one wanted Jim around, not the college, not even the hospital.

Jim's body had responded to treatment. The shaking had stopped. There was nothing wild in his eyes. But they had not been able to reach his mind. His depression was absolute. His thoughts were formless and dark.

Fred heard the swish of a nun's habit and the clack of her rosary beads and recognized the sound of Sister Elizabeth Mary coming down the hall. In a moment she was in the room.

"Cheer up. Cheer up both of you," she said.

She went to Jim's side and took his wrist in her finger tips. The seconds ticked by in silence as she looked at her watch. "You're doing fine," she said and dropped his wrist.

She looked at Fred. Her smile seemed strained, but it was welcome anyway. "He'll be all right and so will you."

Fred rose from the chair and took his coat. "Good-bye Jim. I won't be back to see you. I'm leaving for Detroit tomorrow."

There was no response. Jim continued to stare at the darkness.

"Take care," Fred said.

The nun followed him into the hall. "Good luck on your trip. Don't worry about Father Jim. We'll look after him," she said.

The drunk was nowhere to be seen on the ride back to the college. If he had not gained admission to the Yacht Club, he had wandered off in search of the next drink or a doorway to get out of the wind.

Fred could feel a tide of depression coming in on him. He tried to push it back, but only half-heartedly. It all seemed so futile. This life — it was so hard to face. He was a disgrace, just like Jim. A failed Jesuit. A defeated soldier of Christ. If only a drink was the answer. If only it offered surcease. But it no longer did. He knew that if he picked up a drink, the booze would take over and drag him through days and nights without food and without companionship, through a nightmare where sleep did not refresh and there was no relief, where morning did not bring a new day but a continuation of pain.

Fred felt the need of the night air. He told the cab driver to stop at the main gate to the college so that he could walk to the priests' residence. It was a time for reflection, perhaps even for hope. His life was about to change. He was leaving the college and the students and the Jesuits to go to a place for alcoholic priests outside of Detroit. He did not know how long he would be gone or even if the program would work. He suspected that it would not. But he wanted to try it. It was his last chance.

He had not had a drink since just after the holidays. In fact he had almost made it through the holidays without a drink. He had gotten through Thanksgiving and exams and made it to the Christmas vacation when the campus was almost empty and the priests were most relaxed. It was a good time, there was a special peace and camaraderie. Fred enjoyed it, as much as he was able to, and then on

Christmas Eve, without any premeditation, he had a drink. And this time it was worse than it had ever been. He was out of control, and a part of him detached and watched as he slid into the abyss, as his moral fiber disintegrated. He had set out to be a priest, a teacher, a man of God. Now those things were lost to him. He was a bad man and a bad priest. He was a drunkard in a Roman collar. He wondered if there was anything worse than a priest lying on the floor with a bottle in his hand — especially at Christmas when the great body of Christianity celebrated the Nativity.

While the other priests enjoyed themselves, he was a shadow in the hall, slinking to his room, a bottle hidden against the side of his leg. He tried to be unobtrusive, tried to escape these men. His presence was unwelcome to the other priests and even to himself. But there was no escape. Alcohol dulled the pain and the shame, but it did not remove them.

He came out of it on the second of January. He was sweaty and shaking and full of anxiety and fear, but he had found a new resolve. A friend had told him about the program for alcoholic priests, and he was ready to try it. Everything else had failed. Prayer, discipline, promises, vows, pledges, determination. Nothing worked. It was time for drastic measures.

At first his superiors could not see why Fred needed to go away. Willpower was all that was needed. Right reason. A man should be able to pick up a drink or put a drink down or stay away from it altogether.

In the end it was Father Charlie who interceded for him. He convinced the dubious superiors to let Fred try the program, and they reluctantly agreed. Fred applied to the place which was called Guest House, and to his dismay he was told he would have to wait two months to get in. It was like sitting on a time bomb. He was afraid that sooner or later he would take another drink. He did not want to. But he knew that it was not a question of wanting or not wanting. He knew that alcohol was stronger than he was.

Fortunately, Charlie was there, and Charlie watched Fred like a hawk. But it was a grim period, like serving out a prison term. Nothing could happen until the time was up. And now it was. He was ready to leave. As Fred approached the priests' residence his depression left him. It was replaced by stirrings of elation. He was about to start on an adventure. He was about to do something about his drinking.

"Been up to see Jim?" a voice asked from the shadows. It was Charlie.

Fred nodded.

"Any better?"

"He looks — well — he looks a little better. But he's the same. I don't even know if he's aware that I come to see him."

"Give him time, Fred."

"He's had time."

"Well, give him some more."

Chapter Two

It was very lonely at night. Sounds seemed isolated and far off, and they made him feel isolated and far off, too. When he heard the quick footsteps of a nurse in the hall, he would long for her to come into his room. But usually the footsteps would fade down the corridor, and he would sink further into the dark abyss of his loneliness. It was awful not being able to sleep. The anxieties, the fear, the memories — they crowded into his bed and into his brain. How could anyone sleep in that bedlam of past and future, of pain and shame and despair? Sleep was the great restorer. It brought health and relief. But to get to sleep, one had to cross through a period of utter relaxation where the brain was not directed, where it was free to skip and buzz and flit across the conscious and unconscious — and it was that period which terrified him. Just when he would begin to drift off, a sudden memory or a wild half-formed thought would pierce his repose. His body would snap, as if it had been jolted by an electrical shock, and he would be fully awake again, mind racing, heart pounding, body sweating, like a child after a nightmare — only the nightmare did not end upon awakening.

Sometimes when he awoke, Sister Liz Mary would be there to comfort him and to ease the terror of the night. She was a blessing. Most of the time, however, he would awaken alone. He would lie in the darkness, his pajamas soaked with perspiration, and he would be besieged by fear. It was not a specific fear. It was not the fear of death or of the dark or of anything in particular. It was just fear. A great ogre against which he was helpless. He would fight it by groping for a pleasant thought or a consoling memory. There was one special memory that helped to calm him, and when his brain was not too paralyzed by fear and he had the presence of mind to summon it, the memory would come to him as fresh as yesterday. Cool evenings on Kaiser Island — a combination vacation retreat and Jesuit Siberia in the Long Island Sound. It was a place for priests to get away and relax in the summer, and it was also a place where the order sent problem priests to take them out of circulation and give them some time to get their lives back in order.

It was on Kaiser Island that his friendship with Fred had begun. They were both in trouble. Their lives were shattered and their careers were in disarray. They had gravitated to each other, perhaps because they knew that in each other's company they were free from criticism, even the unspoken kind. Gradually, like prisoners thrown together in the same cell, they had opened up to each other, and one night as they sat by the water surveying the ruins of their lives, Fred, who was a theologian, interrupted one of his interminable silences. "Jim, it's God who's doing this to us," he said.

Jim had been struck by the thought, and he clung to it. It gave him the slimmest hope that his suffering and humiliation were not for naught. If God was doing this to him, perhaps his life was not senseless. It was a small consolation, but it was the only one he had. Still, as he lay on the bed sweating in the darkness, he could not help but wonder just what it was that God had in mind.

They told him that he was getting better, that he would be all right. He must have been very sick. He did not remember coming to the hospital. In fact, he did not remember exactly when he started to remember. He had come out of a great fog bank. There had been a voice here and a face there — his brother, Sister Liz Mary, his doctor, a nurse's aid — and the slow awareness that he was in the hospital again. Before that he could remember walking across the campus in his pajamas to go to a package store for another bottle. It was winter, but he did not mind the cold. It was dark. No one could see the pajamas under his overcoat, nor could anyone guess that he was wearing slippers. He bought a quart of rye and made it back to his room without being discovered. That was all that he remembered, and even that memory was hazy. They said that Fred had found him. They said he had come to visit every day for weeks. But he did not remember Fred coming. They said his mother had come to see him once, too. He did not remember that either.

Jim awoke with a start. It was light in the room. He must have dozed off. Doctor Brophy was standing against the window reading a chart. Behind him, a mile or so away, Jim could see the hills on the west side of the city. They were green. The winter was over. Life had returned to Massachusetts, and he had missed it.

Doctor Brophy was about the same age as Jim, but a stranger would never have guessed it. Father Jim was frail and emaciated. He looked old and burdened. The doctor, on the other hand, seemed to reflect the season. He was forceful and energetic. Where Jim's expression was vague and doleful, the doctor's was inquisitive and critical. He wore a beautifully tailored grey suit with a paisley bow tie and a white button-down shirt. His hair was just as grey as Jim's, but the doctor's crew cut made the grey less obvious. Everything about him seemed orderly and fastidious. Even the stethoscope which hung from his neck was new. He was precise, professional, and serious, but his presence was kinetic. He seemed to have a vast reservoir of energy at his disposal which he was ready to share with anyone with whom he came in contact. He looked light on his feet, like a tennis player, and Jim felt a tinge of envy. The priest loved tennis, but he had not played in twenty years. He longed for order and precision in his life, but there was none. It seemed so unraveled. Jim felt more than envy; he felt embarrassed by the contrast between himself and the doctor.

Doctor Brophy looked up from the chart. He seemed embarrassed, too and hesitant, as if he wanted to escape his task.

"Well, doctor?" Jim asked, "What's it all about this time?"

The doctor glared at him. For a moment Father Jim thought he saw an uncharacteristic trace of anger.

"We've been over this before, Father Collins." The doctor paused, and the anger left his face. He studied the frail man who dangled his legs from the side of the bed. Like Jim, the doctor was an Irish Catholic. To him priests were special people, especially Jesuits. Doctor Brophy considered them the elite of the Church. He had treated many men in the order. They were all bright. They all had probing minds and sharp wits. Some of them were proud, some of them were distant, but they were all superior.

They were all logicians, and they all intimidated him. Even Father Collins, this emaciated man, was marked by something which approached brilliance. And there was another quality about him which made him seem quite formidable. He had an other worldliness. Doctor Brophy simply could not tell him flat out that he was nothing more nor less than a drunk. And he should not have to. It should be obvious to the priest that he was a drunk. Any sane man in Father Collins' position would know that alcohol was the culprit. But Father Jim really did not seem to understand what his basic problem was. Perhaps all his other afflictions made it impossible for him to see that he was misusing alcohol.

Doctor Brophy studied the chart for a moment. He had been treating the priest for nearly fifteen years, and on several occasions during that time, Jim had almost died. And during that time there had not been one day that the priest had been free from pain. Jim had been sick since the days when he was a young seminarian. It had started with a bad back and came to encompass a whole series of physical ailments. He had experienced a great deal of pain, and along the way, he had become addicted to the pain medications and sleeping pills which had been prescribed for him. The priest consumed pills the way greedy children eat candy. It had finally caught up with him — alcohol, drugs, physical degeneration. He had been laid waste.

What could the doctor tell this fragile human being? That he was a drunk? And even if he did tell him, would it help or would it merely serve to embarrass both men. The doctor knew, of course, that the American Medical Association now held that alcoholism was a disease. That seemed a humane position for the AMA. Labeling drunkenness a disease could be a comfort to the sufferer and to his family, but to Doctor Brophy disease was something that could be examined under a microscope or cut out with a knife; it was not something which involved human choice.

Of course, the priest was sick, but as far as the doctor was concerned, Father Jim was sick because he had chosen to drink, much like the child who gets sick because he chooses to stuff himself on pie and ice cream. The priest was a victim of his own indulgence. It was an indulgence that had become habitual, but it was still a habit that was a consequence of his own weak personality, his own lack of will power.

Doctor Brophy weighed his choices. He could try to explain to the priest that his problem was alcoholism. If he thought that Father Jim would accept and act on that diagnosis, then the doctor would have no compunction about risking the potential embarrassment to them both. But the doctor knew that he could predict the priest's response — Father Jim would be insulted and deny any suggestion of alcoholism. The doctor would have alienated the priest to no good purpose. On the other hand, if Doctor Brophy was not forthright with Father Jim, the priest would most certainly drink again and that would mean either death or a damaged brain and permanent institutionalization. But he would drink again, no matter what the doctor told him. Doctor Brophy knew that. It was the alcoholic's pattern. They just did not listen. It would do absolutely no good to tell this poor shrunken man that he was a drunkard. Only a sadist would do that. It was regrettable; it might even be tragic, but it was not an isolated case. He had met other priests who were drunkards, but he had never met one who had overcome his affliction. It was a case of once a priest, always a priest and once a drunk, always a drunk. In all the years he had been practicing medicine, he had had only one patient who was able to escape a serious drinking problem. The man was a plumber who joined Alcoholics Anonymous. The doctor knew nothing about the organization, and the fact that it worked for one man, a man who was not a professional, did not seem enough to recommend it to a Jesuit priest. He could imagine the consternation in the diocesan offices if it got around that he had sent a priest to A.A.

Doctor Brophy looked up from the chart. "Father Collins, you have been through a great trauma. It has had a devastating effect on your body and on your mind. No one blames you for it. We know your medical history. When I review your records, it's like looking over the records of a ward full of patients, never mind one man."

It was true. The priest had suffered a great deal, and some of the suffering had probably been Doctor Brophy's fault. For a number of years, in addition to his other problems, Father Jim had complained of severe stomach pains. He had been checked and rechecked. X-rays failed to show anything. The GI series was always negative. Despite the medical evidence, the priest continued to insist that he was sick and in pain until, finally, they wrote him off as a hypochondriac and sent him to a psychiatrist to find out why he was imagining his discomfort. The ulcers were there, however, hidden where the small intestine meets the stomach. They were discovered at the insistence of a nun who persisted in believing Father Jim when everyone else doubted him. During one of the priest's attacks, she arranged for one last test, and it was this test which clearly showed the presence of the ulcers. He was operated on, and the ulcers were removed. But treating the priest was like handling fly paper. There was always another sticking point. As a result of the operation, perhaps complicated by his continued drinking, Father Jim suffered from the dumping syndrome. Shortly after eating, he would become weak and break out in a sweat. He would suffer acute distress as his meal was dumped from the stomach to the bowel without being digested. Sometimes the syndrome clears up by itself, but not in Father Jim's case. He suffered as much now, perhaps even more, than he had with the ulcers.

Doctor Brophy wondered what kept the priest alive. Other men would have long since gone to their reward. He looked like a victim of a concentration camp. His pajamas billowed around his shrunken frame — and yet, there was a spark there. It was in his smile, when he could muster a smile, and it reflected an intensity in him — a commitment to life. Perhaps, the doctor thought, he would have been better without it. He would have died earlier, but he would have suffered less.

Doctor Brophy decided to take the plunge.

"The fact is, Father, your condition has been seriously aggravated by your use of alcohol and by the drugs you have taken. Your body no longer tolerates those chemicals. For years you were able to drink and take medications and snap back from it, but now the elastic has gone out of your system. You don't snap back. I'm afraid that another bout like the one you've been through will kill you."

The priest stared at the doctor, but he did not speak.

"For you to get better, you will have to stay away from alcohol and the medications you've been taking."

Father Jim looked somewhat incredulous. He understood what the doctor was saying, but he also knew that what the doctor was proposing was impossible. At a very deep level Father Jim knew that alcohol was as essential to him as oxygen. To say that he could not drink was the same thing as saying he would have to stop breathing. And pills — pills got him through the times between drinks.

"What about my pain?" he asked.

"There is no easy answer to that, Father Collins. I appreciate the discomfort that you experience with your bowel problems, but perhaps in time that will get better.

Right now, however, medication will only compound your problems. We simply can't give you anything for pain."

"Does that mean I'm just going to have to learn to live with this?" Father Jim's voice was sad and filled with despair.

Doctor Brophy ignored the priest's tone.

"That is just what it means. At least for now. You won't always have the pain. Your recovery has been slow, and it will continue to be slow. But you are recovering. Once you get some weight on that frame, you will feel a lot better."

Father Jim brightened. He looked like a man who had found a ray of hope. "Eating has never been my strong suit, Doctor. It is going to be very difficult for me to put weight on. I just don't have the appetite, and about the only thing that has ever stimulated it has been a drink before dinner."

There was a long silence in the room. The two men stared straight into each other's eyes. Neither blinked. Finally, the doctor spoke.

"You know, Father, there is nothing wrong with a drink or two before dinner. There is absolutely nothing wrong with that — if that is all there is."

"You mean, if I had a drink or two before dinner to aid my digestion, it would be all right?"

The doctor became formal and his speech bordered on being sharp. "If you will hold it to one or at the most two drinks before dinner — and nothing more — I don't see anything wrong. But let me emphasize this — if you fall back into heavy drinking, you will end up dead."

Father Jim nodded vigorously in agreement. Suddenly the day seemed much brighter, spring seemed more alive. Already the months in darkness and the pain were receding in his memory.

"Certainly, Doctor, certainly. A drink or two before dinner. Nothing more."

Doctor Brophy had a few other things to say, but Father Jim barely paid attention. He was getting out. He would leave the hospital in a day or two, and he could have a drink or two before dinner. Game, set, and match to Collins. It was late spring. The students would be leaving soon. He would have the whole summer to rest and get back his health. It was exhilarating, positively exhilarating.

When the doctor left, Jim found some stationery and wrote a short note to Fred who was now at the place outside of Detroit for alcoholic priests.

"Dear Fred," he wrote, "Things are looking up. They're finally letting me out of the hospital. By the time you receive this, I will have returned to the campus for a leisurely period of convalescence. The doctor says I'm a lot better and should continue to improve. He even says that I can have a drink or two before dinner. Should help me to put a little weight on. Hope things are going well for you. All the best. Jim."

A few days later, he got a short note from Fred.

"Jim — Why don't you come out to Guest House? Miracles are happening out here. Fred."

Chapter Three

The ride to Boston was long and silent. Jim sat in the back seat with Bill Donahue, the president of the college. Charlie Connell, who apparently thought of himself as a guardian angel for drunken Jesuits, drove. They got off the Massachusetts Turnpike where it ended at Route 128 in Newton. From there to Logan Airport the traffic was torturously slow. Whenever they stopped for a red light, Jim thought about bolting from the car and running to a bar for a drink. But it was pure fantasy. There was no sprinting in him. He could barely walk. The last bender had been the ne plus ultra drunk of his life. He remembered very little about it. He had, according to Father Donahue, picked up a retinue, and they had jumped from bar to bar across the central and western parts of the state. They had even journeyed (by taxi which was charged to the college) into Connecticut. Jim had held forth on all subjects and had tried to instruct the company in rudimentary Latin so that they could order drinks at any Jesuit house in the world.

There had been women, according to Donahue, who now sat staring out of his window without uttering a sound. Of course, there had been women, Jim thought. Not to sleep with, though. Just for company. He loved women. He loved their conversation, he loved their charm, he loved their company. But drunk or not, he was a priest, and he was celibate, whether Bill Donahue wanted to believe that or not. For just a moment, a feeling of self-righteousness began to grow in Jim. Imagine, he thought, them thinking that I would break my vow of celibacy? Imagine. What kind of Jesuit do they think I am?

The realization came crashing in on him. They thought he was a failure, a bum, a man who should never have been admitted to the Jesuits. He was, they said, a cause of scandal. He was an embarrassment to the society. He should never have become a priest.

At one of the bars, there was a fat man, really huge. He drank and ate like a debauched Roman. But curiously, he seemed to understand. He took a liking to Jim and sat with him and talked. They had shared their histories. Jim could not remember what either of them had said. Had it all been lies? Had it been truthful? He could not recall. But he had an affinity with the man. They were brothers under the skin. Suddenly he remembered what the man had told him.

"I've been out of control since I was ten, but I never admitted it until I was forty. Now I'm like a big piece of driftwood. I go with the tide and the currents. Sometimes I damage unsuspecting vessels, and sometimes I wind up on the beach. I never know what's going to happen. I just sort of drift."

"What wonderful insight you have," Jim told the man whose name he could not remember. "That's very noble.

To know yourself — that's the beginning of wisdom. Or the end. One or the other. I can't remember which. But it's very wise."

"You're like that, too," the man said. "You're a skinny piece of driftwood. But I bet you've sunk a few ships in your time."

"This is a lark," Jim told him. "Just a lark. I'm convalescing. I've been very, very ill."

That fat man laughed. "Yeah, well it doesn't look like you're recuperating too well either. And this isn't the way priests usually recuperate anyway. Are you really a priest?"

Jim nodded.

"Say something in Latin."

Jim thought for a moment, and then he quoted the inscription above the entrance to the college library. "Ut cognoscant te solum deum verum et quem misisti Jesum Christum."

"What does it mean?"

"It's just a motto that we have," Jim said.

"Yeah," the man answered. "To know the one true God and Jesus Christ whom he sent."

"It was the only thing that came to mind," Jim said.

The man nodded. "I guess this isn't eternal life, huh?"

The fat man's gentle irony was like an accusing finger. Where do men like that come from? Jim wondered. Was he real or was he a hallucination? He seemed real. They had been in a bar in Barre or was it in Ware? As mulled as he was, Jim had still felt the vague blush of shame. Now he remembered the quote in full. It was from John's gospel. Jesus said it just before he was arrested. "And this is eternal life: To know the one true God and Jesus Christ whom he sent."

Going into the Sumner Tunnel was like descending into Purgatory. The artificial light, the yellow walls, the downward pitch. No bars down here. No chance to bolt. Ride it out. Ride out the storm. Three silent Jesuits riding out the storm.

"Flight 107 for Detroit now boarding."

The words lifted a pall from the three men. Jim avoided looking in their eyes as he shook hands with his fellow priests. After very brief good-byes he took his light travelling bag and started through the boarding gate. The other two priests turned to go, but Bill Donahue changed his mind, and instead of leaving, they stood by the gate and chatted.

As he looked back, a feeling of utter humiliation returned to Jim. These men had been his friends. Now he was a burden to them. His career was over. He used to fly around the country giving talks and attending conferences. Now he was reduced to the role of an erring child to be looked after at airports and guarded until he could be safely deposited somewhere else with someone else to look after him and keep him out of trouble.

Shortly after they were aloft, a stewardess was at his seat. "Hi, Father. Can I get you something? Coffee and a danish?"

She was young and splendid in her uniform, not a hair out of place. She made Jim feel like he had been restored to the human race.

"I'd love it," he answered with a smile.

It was a mistake, of course. Within fifteen minutes, he was writhing in pain. His fingers dug into the armrests and his brow was covered with perspiration.

"Father, are you all right?"

The stewardess put her hand on his shoulder and leaned close to him.

"It's an intestinal problem," he said. "It will pass."

"Anything I can do."

His escort was gone, and he was in severe pain. The woman was compassionate, treating him like an adult and not like a willful child. For the moment he was free. It wouldn't last, of course. It would end when the plane landed.

"Yes, I think a drink would help."

She nodded sympathetically.

"What would you like, Father?"

He hesitated. He would have preferred not to have a drink, but, in fact, he needed one. No debate. No recriminations.

"I'll have a scotch. Put it in a tall glass, please."

She glided away, and in a moment she was back with a very large scotch.

"Remember, Father, one in the air is worth three on the ground," she said.

"It better be," he thought.

He felt the scotch slide down his throat and into his ruined stomach. There was a sudden soothing warmth. His physical anguish abated, and the tension began to drain from his body. Bill and Charlie were driving back to the college. They were probably talking about him. He could almost hear them. But what did they know — really? Could they understand the pain? Could they understand the interior unraveling? Or the special need that he had for alcohol? It was, for him, a medicine, a pain reliever. It restored an interior unity. It stilled the screaming voices. They could not understand that because they were not torn by the pain and by the concomitant angst. Yes, that was it. Angst. As much as he disagreed with the existentialists. Catholic or otherwise, he knew angst when he felt it, and he knew that a tall glass of scotch took it away.

He looked out the window and was impressed by how orderly the landscape seemed. The roads neatly bisected the fields as if following a master plan. Rivers, railroad tracks, all seemed to have their place. It was quite unlike the complete disorder of his life.

He had taken it easy when he first got out of the hospital. Two drinks before dinner. That was it. Later that week, he had a couple before he went to bed to help him sleep. Within a few days he was drinking almost around the clock. This time, though, the other priests kept an eye on him, and they shipped him off to a drying out place before he could cause himself too much trouble. Had he been there once that summer or twice? He could not remember. It was a very pleasant spot on a lake in the northern part of the state, run by a rather striking woman. It was surrounded by woods and away from everything. They let him down easy and he loved it. Nice people. Nice staff. A haven. There had even been moments when it was fun.

That was before the final bender.

"Fred is doing very well out at Guest House," Bill Donahue had told him. "In fact, we're going to let him stay out there for a while. He's doing some kind of biography. I'm not sure exactly how it all works. But he's being helped. We contacted this man Ripley out there about you, and he's willing to let you go out and try it. He says it's not too late for you to come out there. In fact, according to Ripley, there are no hopeless cases."

"Believe it or not," Jim said.

Father Donahue merely stared at him.

Chapter Four

*J*im had barely struggled out of the car when the man grabbed him in a bear hug. "Welcome to Guest House, Father Collins. I'm Austin Ripley." Next to Jim, the man was a behemoth. He was large without being overweight. He looked like an older athlete who refused to get out of shape. And on top of that he was a very smart dresser. Just looking at him, Jim felt at a disadvantage.

"It's wonderful to have you here, Father. Wonderful that you could come."

Jim was at a loss for words so he just nodded.

He was standing in front of an imposing Tudor mansion. It reminded him of Shadowbrook in the Berkshires and his days as a seminarian. The huge house was set back at least five hundred feet from the road giving it a regal air. The grounds were meticulously kept. This was a place for the rich, for the elite, for the chosen, and he was dimly conscious that Ripley was treating him as if he was one of the elite, one of the chosen.

"John," he called to the driver, "Please take Father Collins' bags." Then he turned to Jim. "Let's get out of this chill," Ripley said.

It was a crisp autumn day, but Ripley did not look cold. He seemed full of energy and inner warmth. He wore a tweed sports jacket, a striped tie with a blue button-down shirt, tan slacks and white shoes. A white handkerchief billowed from the breast pocket of his jacket. Even his bald head seemed well groomed and vigorous. If Ripley seemed perfectly comfortable, Jim did not. The scotch had worn off hours ago, and Jim could feel the chill despite his black topcoat and hat.

The inside of the mansion was as impressive as the outside. It was warm and bright, and as he sat sipping coffee in Ripley's office, Jim was relieved. This was not at all like being in jail.

"Let me acquaint you with a few basics," Ripley said. "We're on your side here. Everybody who works at Guest House has recovered from alcoholism. And that includes me. This is not an ecclesiastical prison. And you are not here to do penance. You are here to get well and to learn how to live again."

Jim mustered the trace of a smile. "You're pretty good at mind reading," he said.

Ripley laughed. "We've had a lot of priests come here. Most of them have been in trouble with their superiors. Many of them in fact have been in what amounted to ecclesiastical prisons. Prisons don't help alcoholics. They're prisoners already. They're prisoners inside of themselves. What we try to do here is set them free."

He leaned back and spun his swivel chair so that he could look out the window at the rolling lawns and then he swung around again to examine Jim.

"How was the plane ride?"

"Not bad."

"Did you have a drink?"

"A couple of scotches."

"How do you feel now?"

"Like I need another one."

"A little edgy?" Ripley asked.

"More than a little," Jim replied.

"All right. We'll just take a couple of more minutes, ask a few questions, and then we'll get you into our little hospital and detoxify you — that's one of those fancy words the Romans picked up from the Greeks. It means we'll get the poison out of your system. I forget, of course, that I'm talking to a man who studied the classic languages. Forgive me."

Jim shrugged.

Ripley opened a file folder which lay on his desk and picked up a pen. "What brought you here, Father?"

Jim seemed a little confused. "American Airlines."

Ripley laughed loudly. "I mean what made you decide to come to Guest House?"

"My superiors. We take a vow of obedience. They say go and you go."

"Were you having problems?"

"I've had problems for a long time," Jim said.

"Ah," Ripley replied. He put the pen down and leaned back in his chair.

"I've been in chronic pain with my back since I was seventeen. For years I had stomach ulcers that they couldn't find. So they thought I was crazy and sent me to a psychiatrist. Now, as a result of getting rid of the ulcers they screwed something else up. Whenever I eat, I have incredible distress because I don't digest the food. Yes, Mr. Ripley, I've had problems. I still have them."

Ripley nodded vigorously.

"Yes, I can see that. How old are you, Father?"

"Fifty."

Ripley's eyebrows arched. Jim did not look a day under seventy.

"Among the problems that you've had, was one of them a problem with booze?"

"Some people seem to think so. My bosses think so. That's for sure."

"How about you?"

"I don't know."

Ripley did not respond.

"I've had a lot of problems. I've had a lot of pain. Alcohol has been a help to me over the years. It eased the pain. It let me sleep."

Ripley leaned forward and looked closely at the priest. He seemed old and broken as if there was only half a spark of life in him. The pain and the confusion were written in the lines of his face and there was something else there as well. Ripley had seen it thousands of time. Years earlier, he had seen it in himself although he did not recognize it then.

To any rational person, it would be obvious that Father Jim had a serious problem with alcohol. Whatever other problems he may have had, there was empirical evidence that alcohol had very nearly turned him into a vegetable and very nearly killed him. It was responsible for making him an outcast in his order, for ruining his priesthood, alienating his family and friends, and turning him into a prematurely old man, really just a shattered husk of a human being. But the Reverend James D. Collins S.J., for all his knowledge of history and philosophy, psychology and theology and the classics, could not see that alcohol was the culprit in his life. Instead, he saw it as his friend. He was a victim of alcoholic denial. It was part of his disease. And as long as he could not make the connection between his drinking and his problems he would never be able to get well. It was that simple.

Without intending to, Ripley threw up his hands.

Jim, despite his discomfort, picked up on it immediately.

"That bad, huh?"

Ripley slowly smiled and then he laughed rather loudly but good-naturedly.

"You're not the worst case I've seen. There are a few obstacles in your path. But the body's still warm."

"Not very," Jim said hunching his shoulders together.

"Maybe it's not very warm, but there's still a pulse. And I don't believe on giving up on priests with booze problems until they're dead — or they've got wet brains."

He gave Jim a moment to let that sink in, and then he rose from his chair.

"Come on. I'll bring you to our little hospital section, and we'll start you back on the road to life."

Chapter Five

"Why is it that nobody around here understands? Jim looked directly at Fred, but Fred had turned and was staring out the window.

The world outside looked cold and antiseptic. It had snowed during the night, and the morning sun's brilliance was blinding. But even though his eyes hurt, Fred preferred looking out the window rather than turning to Jim.

"Nobody seems to understand that I am in pain. Nobody seems to care. 'That's all right, Father Jim. It will get better.' 'Shut up and listen, Father Jim. It works for us; it will work for you.' 'Take the cotton out of your ears and put it in your mouth, Father Jim.' That's bullshit, Fred, and you know it and I know it. I am listening. I'm going to as many A.A. meetings a week as anybody in North America. I literally go morning, noon and night. My life is one long A.A. meeting. 'Put the plug in the jug.' 'Don't drink and go to meetings. — It's the first drink that gets you drunk. — Live and let live. — Easy does it. — Let go and let God .— One day at a time.' I've heard it all. I don't think there is another organization in the world with so many slogans. 'Sit up front.' 'Identify and don't compare.' 'If you don't drink you can't get drunk.' "

"They work, Jim," Fred said.

"Not for me," Jim said sharply. "Not for me. Tell my stomach they work. Tell my aching back they work. And then tell me they work. They're a bunch of platitudes. A class of fourth-graders could come up with better lines than those."

"Well, they're working for me," Fred said.

"Maybe," Jim answered. "But we don't have the same problems. I mean you really haven't experienced what I've experienced. You haven't been sick most of your life. Look at me. A strong breeze would blow me over. And because I took a vow of obedience, I have to come to this place. I mean, I have given up everything. I gave up a regular life — my brother's a doctor, I could have had a career — I gave up women, I gave up money, I gave up everything that can be given up. And on top of it, I'm sick. And they treat me like a skid row case, like I'm some kind of pariah that can't be kept around their precious Jesuit community. I'm as good as any Jesuit that ever lived, when I'm well. Can't the bastards see that I'm sick?"

"Jim, they know you're sick. Believe me," Fred said.

"Well, they're not doing a hell of a lot about it."

"They're trying, Jim."

Fred looked at his watch and sighed. There were only a couple of minutes before the morning session began. That was a comfort. If only Jim would keep his mouth shut for those few minutes. Fred had looked forward to Jim's arrival. He had prayed for it. Indeed, he had longed for it. And now he was reminded of another A.A. expression.

"Be careful what you pray for, you may get it." Fred had received what he prayed for and more. Once Jim had gotten out of the detoxification unit, he had developed an unending litany of complaints. At every free moment, Jim would rattle off all of his troubles and all the faults of the Jesuits, of Guest House, and of life in general. Fred was a man easily given to depression and doubt, and he was often convinced that he would never be able to get better. Only rarely did he see a ray of hope, but whenever he did, Jim would unfailingly shroud it in darkness. Now, Fred wanted to get away from him, but he did not know how to do it.

"Time to start," a voice called.

Fred was grateful. His ordeal with Jim was over for at least an hour. He and Jim found adjoining seats in a large room which had been turned into a classroom complete with blackboards and desk-chairs. Austin Ripley stood next to a gray office desk at the front of the room. He smiled, nodded, and, occasionally, winked as about twenty men, all of whom wore Roman collars, found their seats.

"Good morning, gentlemen," Ripley said in a hearty voice.

"Good morning, Rip," a priest sitting in the front row answered.

Ripley nodded to him.

"Gentlemen, for the past week or so, I've been giving you the science of alcoholism, what we know about the disease, which isn't too much, and how it works. We've talked about the mental obsession with alcohol and the physical compulsion to drink it that the active alcoholic has. We've talked about the progression of the disease. We've talked about the human metabolism, how alcohol enters the blood stream, how the liver works, the effect of alcohol on the brain, we've talked about addiction and withdrawal and denial. And you're going to hear a lot more about all of those things. But this morning, I thought we'd do something a little bit different."

Ripley looked down at the handkerchief in his left breast pocket and made a slight adjustment to it. He was a very dapper fellow, a clothes horse, given to changing his outfit two or three times a day. Jim found that rather bizarre, and it was one of the things he often mentioned to Fred. This morning Ripley was wearing a blue jacket with grey slacks and shining penny loafers. His shirt was a brilliant white, and his tie was a conservative pinstripe.

"When I was new to sobriety, I'd look around at some of the people who got here before me, and I'd wonder about them. 'They don't look like alcoholics,' I'd think to myself. 'How did they get here?'

"And I'm sure that one or two of you, maybe all of you, have had those thoughts about me. 'Ripley doesn't look like a drunk,' you may have said to yourself. 'The man is a fashion plate. He dresses too well to be a drunk,' you've probably said."

The room filled with laughter.

" 'A high-bottom drunk,' you have probably thought. Well, I thought this morning that I would set the record straight — tell you a little about myself, my drinking history — or drunk-a-log as a lot of people call it — and how I got to be where I am today."

Fred snuck a glance at Jim. He looked like he was paying attention.

"I was a writer," Ripley began. "I wrote for Look magazine and a number of other publications. I suppose some people would think of my life as glamorous. I had a wife who starred in movies. I had a successful career. Things on the outside looked pretty good. But I had something working against me. I liked to drink, and when you're a writer and your time is your own, there are lots of opportunities.

You don't have to wait until the sun is over the yardarm. You often have the house to yourself. My wife used to go to work very early and get home pretty late. And I would start drinking whenever I felt like it, and after a while I pretty much felt like it all the time.

"Things got worse for me. The people we hurt the most are the ones closest to us. That was true in my case. My wife got sick of dealing with a drunk, and one day, in a huff, I left. I started to travel around the country, and, of course, I eventually ran out of money — I was in Chicago at the time — and I hit the skids. But, you know, the alcoholic mind is really inventive. And I told myself that I was on skid row to do research. I could see the headlines: 'Chicago's Seamy Side: Writer Takes First-Hand Look at Skid Row.'

"After a while, my wife and a friend came looking for me. It took them a long time, but they finally found me, and when they did, they asked me what I was doing living like a bum, and I told them. 'Research.' "

Again, the room swelled with laughter.

"My wife looked at me and she said, 'Rip, you've been doing research for five years. How much more research do you have to do?'

"Five years. Five years. I thought I had only been down there for a couple of months," Ripley said. He waited a moment to let the priests ponder his words.

"Of course, there was a divorce. And I wound up in a charity ward where I heard about A.A. At the time, I really didn't have anything left. I was a wreck physically, and mentally, I could barely connect two thoughts. But I started to go to A.A. meetings and gradually my life began to change. And life is so full of surprises. Any experience can be put to good use. As it turned out, some of the time I spent on skid row really was useful as research. I had met a number of men, drunks like me, who were priests — men who had given their lives to God and had wound up eating in soup kitchens and sucking out of wine bottles in paper bags."

Now there was no laughter. The silence was palpable. The attention strict. Even Jim seemed to be hanging on Ripley's words.

"A couple of years after I came to A.A., I wrote an article about priests on the skids, holy men who were captives of alcoholism. At the time, I was working in Wisconsin, and as a result of the article quite a number of priests who were looking for help, either for themselves or a colleague, looked me up. Finally, an archbishop in St. Paul got a hold of me, and we talked, and he made it clear to me that he understood something about the disease. He knew that alcoholism was not a matter of choice and that drunks were sick people not bad people. So the archbishop asked me to start a full-time program for alcoholic priests. There must have been a market."

Again there was laughter.

"But you see, I had other ideas. I was a writer. In some part of me, I wanted to be the Tolstoy of our age. When I walked down the street, I wanted people to say, 'There goes Austin Ripley, the man who finally wrote the great American novel.' "

He raised his eyebrows and got another laugh.

"So I politely, but firmly, said 'no' to the archbishop. But you see, God had a different plan. I couldn't get the idea out of my mind. I had always had a great respect for people who could give their lives for a noble cause. And it seemed to me that priests were really great heroes, great and dedicated men who had given their lives to the noblest of causes. And I was upset by the way alcoholic priests were being treated. Like lepers, really. They were packed off in disgrace to remote monasteries which did absolutely nothing to help their disease, or they wound up on skid row. The archbishop had said that it was not a very Christian way to treat the sick. He was right. And I could not get the idea out of my mind."

Ripley walked over to the coffee table and poured himself a cup of coffee, took a sip from it and walked back to the desk.

"I was really tortured by the idea. It wouldn't leave me. Well, there's a Trappist monastery near Dubuque and I went over there and spent some time in prayer and reflection. I was in my mid-fifties. My life could not be called a success. I wanted to do more. I wanted to leave this planet having accomplished something. So I prayed and I reflected and I talked to the monks.

"Nobody was doing anything for alcoholic priests. In God's wisdom, I had been given the knowledge and the opportunity to help. In the end, I was convinced that I had been called to serve. Now what I did next, most people are not able to understand. But I think that as priests you will. If you scratch the surface of this eminently dignified gentleman before you," he paused for their laughter, "you will find the soul of a romantic. And the soul of a Catholic. And I decided if I was going to do this thing, it would be an all or nothing proposition. I wouldn't turn back and I wouldn't bail out. I think I have always identified with the Round Table and knights of medieval legend. And I was about to begin a noble adventure — so I solemnly dedicated my life to the Virgin Mary and I entered her service, and I vowed to establish a place where priests could be treated with dignity and with excellent prospects of recovery."

Ripley drained the cup of coffee.

"Well, is that enough about me for today?"

"Finish the story," a priest in the back called out.

"Father George, you've already heard it."

"But it's worth hearing again, Rip."

"All right," Ripley said. "Well, I'm sure all of you gentlemen know what it says in the Book of Wisdom. 'When you set out to serve God, my son, expect obstacles.' Believe me, that is good advice, because about the time that I made my decision, the archbishop — who really put the bee in my bonnet and who was supposed to put up some money for this project — got hit by a car, and he was really in bad shape. The other people in the hierarchy were not so hot on the idea, so suddenly there was no money available. However, all was not lost. Up in Chippewa Falls, Wisconsin, there's a place called St. Joseph's Hospital. And the nuns up there heard about the project and offered to lend me a building. And that's where the first Guest House started. Chippewa Falls — a far cry from Lake Orion.

"Just about the time we opened the doors, all hell broke loose. There were some people in A.A. who felt that the project was opposed to A.A. principles. They thought we were singling out one group of alcoholics for special and exclusive treatment. And, of course, in a way we were. On the other side, there were people in the hierarchy who felt that a layman had no business establishing an institution to take care of priests who they felt were just plain immoral. Rome finally had to decide the case. And we won. But not for long. The local bishop decided he didn't want us around, so he padlocked Guest House and threw us out.

"Can you imagine? I was persona non grata in Chippewa Falls, and I was sober."

Again, Ripley drew prolonged laughter.

"But the Book of Wisdom says to expect obstacles, it doesn't say to expect defeat. If God wants something, he has ways of getting it. In this case, he used Cardinal Mooney in Detroit. The cardinal called me up, invited me out and offered to put up fifty thousand dollars to help buy suitable property. Not bad for a guy who got bounced out of Chippewa Falls.

"But things never go as easy as you hope. We looked all over the Detroit area until finally we found this property in Lake Orion — the Scripps estate. It was built by Scripps of Scripps Howard newspaper fame, but by the time I found it, it was no longer owned by the Scripps family. It was really in bad shape and we had great difficulty even entering into negotiations with the owners. They didn't seem to care, and there was a lot of foot-dragging."

Ripley put his hands in his trouser pockets and surveyed the roomful of priests.

"I don't know whether all of you can understand what happened next, but I'm sure many of you can —especially those who believe in angels. Anybody believe in angels?"

More than half the priests raised their hands.

"Anybody not believe in angels?"

Just a few hands went up.

"Doesn't matter. But I happen to believe in angels. Indeed, I have always considered the arch-angel Raphael to be a good friend of mine. So when it looked like the negotiations would never get off the ground, I took some medals — a miraculous medal, a St. Christopher, and a St. Raphael medal and I snuck onto the property and buried the medals on the grounds. It was at night, and I have never found where I buried them. They're somewhere out toward the front of the property. Too cold to go looking for them now.

"In a very short time, the negotiations got back on track, and we had a home for Guest House. Now I like to think that in some mysterious way, Raphael rolled up his sleeves and went to work so that we could buy this property.

"You see, I believe that God sent Raphael to intervene because he cares about you and is anxious to help you. And I believe that if I hadn't gotten sober, he would have found somebody else to start Guest House.

"But I'm grateful that he found me. And I'm grateful that he found you. Fathers, you will never know how much you, and all who have come before you, have given me."

The session was over, and the men were on their feet slowly filing out the door.

"Father Jim," Ripley called.

Jim stopped and looked back over his shoulder.

"I'd like to see you for a few minutes," Ripley said. "Why don't you get some coffee and meet me in the library?"

Chapter Six

The library was one of Ripley's favorite spots. It was handsomely decorated and filled with expensively bound volumes. The works ranged from Pliny to Fitzgerald, and an avid reader could spend many years in the room reading the best writers and thinkers the world has produced. Ripley did not read nearly as much as he did when he was a young man. But he still enjoyed taking down a volume at random and perusing it. Usually, he found something interesting or profound, but he was rarely able to read more than a paragraph or two without being interrupted. When Jim entered the room, he found Ripley sitting in a high-backed chair thumbing through a rather large volume. Ripley jumped up and placed the book back on a shelf.

"Sit down, Father, please," he said.

Jim looked at Ripley warily. He had had enough interviews with his superiors to sense when there was something in the wind that he might not like. He strained to see the title of the volume that Ripley had returned to the shelf, hoping to get a clue as to the reason for the interview. It was Plutarch's "Lives."

"How are you feeling?" Ripley asked once Jim was seated.

Jim bent his head and looked at Ripley over his glasses. "Lousy."

"How are you sleeping at night?"

"I'm not."

"What about eating?

"I don't."

"I believe you," Ripley said.

"Thank you."

"Not everybody does, you know."

"I know."

"A lot of people think you're just a chronic complainer."

"I know."

"But you're not."

"No."

The exchange had been rapid-fire, and when it was over, Ripley smiled. Jim smiled back. It was his first real smile since he had arrived at Guest House.

"There are paradoxes in sobriety," Ripley said. "And one of them is that before you can get better, you have to start to get better. In order to begin recovery, you have to already have some recovery. Do you understand what I'm saying?"

Jim nodded. "There's got to be a foundation. Something to build on."

"Right," Ripley said. "And you don't have that foundation."

Jim nodded again, and slumped in his chair. "You think I'm too sick to get well."

"Right now, yes."

"And you want me to pack my bags," his voice was soft and resigned.

"I'd like that. Yes."

"Now?"

"No. In a day or two just as soon as I can arrange for you to be admitted to a hospital in Detroit."

Jim sat back up.

"What kind of hospital?"

"A medical hospital," Ripley said and smiled. "Not a psychiatric hospital, Father Jim. Alcoholics are not insane in the clinical sense. We're only insane when it comes to booze. You are not a psychiatric case. While you were in the detoxification unit we studied your medical history. And you are one for the medical journals. God alone knows how you have survived all these years. Given what illness has done to you and what you've done to yourself, you should have been dead a long time ago. I think we can attribute your continued presence to the grace of God operating in your life."

Jim snorted. "Some grace. Some life," he said.

Ripley looked surprised.

"I'm a prisoner," Jim said. "I'm a prisoner in this place, and I'm a prisoner inside my own body. I can't remember what it is like to go a day without pain. I can't remember what it's like to sleep without booze or pills. I can't remember what it's like to eat with enjoyment. I used to be able to drink. And that would take care of the pain. It would let me sleep. It would give me respite. But now I've developed what you call 'an allergy of the body' to booze, and I can't even drink."

Ripley nodded. "Sometimes life deals us a tough hand."

"Tough hand? Is that what you call it?"

"That's right," Ripley said, "And we can either feel sorry for ourselves or we can do something about it."

"Like what. I've tried to do everything that has been suggested here, and none of it has done any good."

"I know," Ripley said. "That's why I'm suggesting that you go into the hospital. I've talked to a specialist about you. He thinks that an operation can put an end to all that pain in your bowel as a result of what they so aptly describe as the 'dumping syndrome.' "

"Another operation?"

"Probably."

Jim laughed. "Look at me. Do you really think I could survive another operation?"

"That is the sticking point," Ripley said. "I don't know if you can make it through surgery."

"Then why suggest it?"

"Consider the alternative."

"What alternative? To go on living?" Jim asked.

Ripley shrugged. "With all deference, Father, I'm not sure that your present condition could be termed 'living'."

Jim sat back in his chair, and a look of astonishment crossed his face.

"A few years ago, Father, I was having trouble with a molar. It became infected. It abscessed. And it caused me an incredible amount of pain. I called the dentist in the afternoon, and his receptionist made an appointment for me at nine the next morning. You can imagine, I'm sure, the agony I was in. Toothaches, at least for me, are one of the most difficult kinds of pain to deal with.

"Anyway, late that afternoon, I left the building and went outside — trying to walk the pain off, I guess, and I ran into a few fellows who were standing around watching the sun set. They were rhapsodic about it. 'Rip,' they kept saying, 'look at those colors. Look at that purple and the crimson. Look at that cloud formation. Look at the way the rays stream across the sky.'

"I didn't appreciate any of it. I just wanted them to shut up and leave me alone. A man with a severe toothache can only think about the toothache. It requires all his mental energy. There is nothing left to appreciate the beauty of nature.

"Right now, Father, you cannot appreciate life or its purpose. There is no joy for you. There is no peace. There is no hope. As it stands, recovery seems unobtainable. Your physical pain engages all your energy. There is nothing left to pursue health."

"So it's a case of do or die," Jim said. "Or maybe do and die."

"Yes, I suppose it is," Rip said.

An awkward silence fell on the room. The two men alternately stared at each other and looked away.

Jim struggled to his feet. "Do I get some time to think or are you just going to hustle me off in an ambulance?"

"Father, the choice is yours. I'm not twisting your arm. I'm just clarifying your situation. If you don't want the operation, don't have the operation. But before you make a decision, why don't you pray about it? Think about it, and pray about it."

Jim sighed heavily. He did not want to admit it, but he was not sure that he could trust God.

Jim had no sooner left the library and Ripley then he met Fred, but he was so concerned with himself that he failed to notice the pained look on Fred's face when he approached him.

"I just saw Ripley," Jim said. "He wants me to have another operation. Can you believe it?"

Fred did not answer.

"They never let up."

"Neither do you," Fred said, quietly.

"They just never let up," Jim said, ignoring him.

"And neither do you," Fred said very deliberately and with just a trace of anger.

This time Jim noticed. "What do you mean, 'neither do I?' "

"Just what I said. Since you have come out here, we have not had one single conversation that you did not talk about yourself and the way you are being mistreated. You are a classic broken record."

Jim looked shocked. Fred's strong suit was meekness. It was very much out of character for him to be so critical.

"Every time I begin to see a ray of hope, you come around and pull the shades. You're like a black cloud. All you can think about is yourself. You don't think about me. You don't think about the other men. It's all Jim. You're the only person that exists. No one else and nothing else matters."

"Well," Jim started to speak, but Fred silenced him.

"I've thought about this quite a bit. I've gone over it and over it in my mind. You are my best friend. But your friendship is smothering me."

Now Jim really was shocked. "What do you want me to do?" he asked.

"I am naturally despondent. And you feed into that. I think that talking to you impedes my recovery. As much as this pains me, I think we have to stay away from each other."

"What?"

"I'm sorry, but I want to get well. I don't think you do. I think you would rather complain."

— ✧ —

Jim spent the afternoon in silence. He felt utterly humiliated. Rip had suggested he pray, but only one prayer would come to mind.

"Asperges me, Domine, hysopo, et mundabor: lavabis me, et super nivem dealabor. Miserere mei, Deus, secundum magnam misericordiam tuam."

Jim repeated the prayer over and over in Latin. He wrapped himself in the ancient words which had for him a comforting power. For a long time, he would pray only in Latin, as if that language insulated him from his sin and made it acceptable for him to approach God. But after a while, his mind began to dwell on the prayer in English. "Sprinkle me, Lord, with hyssop, and I shall be clean: wash me, and I will be made whiter than snow. Have mercy on me, God, according to your great mercy."

And then, finally, he remembered another part of that same psalm. "Cor mundum crea in me, Deus: et spiritum rectum innova in visceribus meis. — A clean heart create in me, God, and a proper spirit renew in my innermost part." Except that Jim knew that visceribus was sometimes translated bowel. "Create a clean heart in me and a proper spirit renew in my bowel."

For more than an hour he prayed first in Latin and then in English, "Lord, give me a clean heart and a proper spirit in my bowel."

A strange prayer, he thought, but appropriate. He repeated it over and over.

Just before dinner time, he heard them by the window.
"Look at those colors."
"There's a special purple in winter sunsets."
"Magnificent."

He looked out and saw the radiance, and thought, "Who cares?"

Ripley was right. You could not appreciate nature when you had a toothache. You could not appreciate life when your entire attention was focused on your own pain 'in visceribus.'

Ripley was seated behind his desk. He did not seem surprised.

"You're right," Jim said. "I am defined by my pain. I've lost my aesthetic sense."

"You want me to contact the doctor?"

Jim nodded.

"Good," Ripley said, and then noticing that Jim still seemed a bit uncertain, he said, "Father, why don't you just put yourself and the operation in the care of God?"

"Do you think he's to be trusted in cases like these?" Jim asked.

Ripley looked surprised, and then he noticed the hint of a smile on Father Jim's face, and he burst out laughing.

"Give me a clean heart, Lord, and a proper spirit in my bowel," Jim prayed.

Chapter Seven

Harry the Collector was a bit put out. "I don't know why they can't wear civvies," he said. He took the short cigar out of his mouth and inspected the ash. It was cold, but he put the cigar back between his teeth without lighting it.

"This looks more like a meeting of a religious order than it does an A.A. meeting."

Harry was short and wide. He had a bull's neck and a frown which could be intimidating.

"Look at this. There are five guys with black suits and those round collars — what-d'y-call-em collars — on. 'A.A. is not allied with any sect, denomination or institution,' " he quoted.

Jenky nodded. "What do you want to do? You want to throw them out?"

"What d'ya mean throw them out? You can't throw them out," Harry said. "They're alcoholics."

"Then why complain?" Jenky asked.

"I'll tell you why. What about the first-timer that comes here? Suppose you're a Baptist and you just put down a drink and this is your first meeting and you find yourself surrounded by guys in black suits?"

"If I was a Baptist it would confirm my suspicions that a lot of Catholic priests are drunks," Jenky said.

Harry the Collector allowed a small smile to grace his lips.

"Hi," the tall, emaciated priest said. "I'm Father Jim." He shook hands with Jenky and Harry. "Do one of you men have a light?"

Harry lit Jim's cigarette and then lit his own cigar.

"We were just talking about you guys," Harry said.

Jim smiled broadly as if he was expecting a compliment.

"We were wondering why you guys come in your uniforms."

"We're priests," Jim said.

Harry the Collector thought for a moment. "Yeah, but we've got cops here, and firemen. They don't come in their uniforms."

Jim laughed, and the other two men smiled.

"What are your names?"

"They call him Harry the Collector, and I'm Jenky," the taller man said.

"The reason we go out dressed like this is because Ripley tells us to," Jim said.

"He's the guy that runs Guest House," Harry said to Jenky.

"Right. And Rip believes that if a priest sneaks to A.A. meetings in civilian clothes it's like he is denying that he's an alcoholic. A priest is different from other people. Being a priest is not a job, it's a total way of life. And Rip says it is harder for priests to admit they're alcoholics than it is for a lot of other people because priests are supposed to be models. He says that if we dress like priests when people come to us for help but don't dress like priests when we go to get help, then we're hypocrites. And hypocrites don't stay sober."

Harry the Collector examined his cigar. "So you're not out here trying to recruit new Catholics."

Jim exploded with laughter. "We're here for ourselves to learn how to stay sober."

"Well, you've got a head start on the rest of us," Harry said.

Jim was puzzled. "A head start?"

"Sure. You've already got the spiritual side of the program."

Jim nodded and smiled. He did not want to admit that he had not the slightest idea of what Harry was referring to.

"I'm gonna get a cup of coffee before the meeting starts," Jenky said. "You want one, Father?"

"Yes, thanks," Jim said.

He looked around and saw that there were now about fifteen people in the room, five of whom were priests. No wonder Harry was concerned.

"Do you do a lot of twelfth step work, Harry?" Father Jim asked.

"I do some, if I'm asked," Harry said.

"I was wondering because of your nickname. I thought maybe you rounded people up on skid row or something."

"No. A lot of people think that. But no. There are two other guys named Harry who are in A.A. around here. They call me the collector just to keep us separate."

"Oh," Jim said.

"The reason they call me Harry the Collector is that is what I do for a living."

"Now I understand," Jim said. "You're a collector. You collect rare coins or stamps."

"No," Harry replied. "I drive a truck. I'm a garbage collector."

Jenky came back with the coffee.

"Come on, let's get a seat," Harry said.

Jim realized that he was included in Harry's invitation, and he went with the two men to sit up front.

Father Jim made a great effort to listen to the speakers at the meetings he attended, but frequently his mind wandered. A speaker would mention an incident or a place in his past, and without realizing it, Jim would be lost in his own memories, some good, some painful. It was no different this night. A man in a business suit began to tell his story. He spoke of being fired from good jobs, of being thrown out of his home, and ending up in the hospital.

"Father Touch and Go," one of the nurses had dubbed him. And apparently it had been touch and go, although Jim did not remember most of the details. They told him that he had nearly died three times on the operating table. But every time they thought he was finished, life would surge back through him, and the operation would continue.

Later, through the haze, he remembered Ripley and Fred coming to see him. There were tubes going down his nose into his stomach which were extraordinarily uncomfortable, but he refused to complain. He was still angry with Fred and not altogether pleased with Ripley, and he would not give them the satisfaction of calling him a complainer, even though it should be clear to one and all that he had a perfect right to complain.

It had taken him some time to recover. It always did. And then one morning, he realized that he was enjoying his meals. There was no longer any sudden sweating or sharp pain a few minutes after he finished eating. Instead, he would doze off, usually enjoying pleasant half-formed dreams.

Midway through the meeting they took a break and almost everyone got up to get a cup of coffee.

"What d'ya think so far?" Harry the Collector asked Father Jim.

"It's great. It's great," Jim said.

"How long have you been coming?"

"Not very long. I just got out of the hospital a week ago."

"You've only been sober a week?"

"Well, I haven't had a drink in almost two months, but I was in the hospital for quite a while because I needed an operation."

"Oh," Harry said, as if mentally weighing some issue. "How do you like being sober?"

"It's all right," Jim said. "It's pretty quiet, though. Not much drama."

"You used to a lot of drama?" Harry asked.

Jim laughed. "I guess so. Yes."

"You want to see drama, Father? You got tickets on the fifty-yard line to the greatest show on Earth. You keep coming to A.A. and you'll see drama you won't believe."

The final speaker of the night was a shrieker. His voice was high-pitched and loud, and this time Father Jim's mind could not wander.

"People say they're in the doghouse. You hear that. 'I'm in the doghouse,' they say. Let me tell you, I was really in the doghouse more than once. I came home drunk one night — it was pouring out, I mean it was like God turned on this big faucet — and my wife opened the door about two inches and pointed my shotgun right at me. 'You no good such and such,' she says. 'You try to come in this house and they'll be scraping your brains off the sidewalk.'

"Now, my wife's a gentle soul. Really. So when she points a shotgun at you, even if you're drunk out of your mind like I was, you got to take her at her word.

"Now we got this German Shepherd — massive thing, huge — and his name is Himler. Not Hitler. Himler. What can I say? This is a family illness. And he's got this big dog house with a shingled roof and everything that I made for him.

"So I go out to the backyard, and it's raining like crazy, and Himler is all scrunched up in his dog house, and he's looking out at me through the rain, like 'what's going on here?' You know how dogs are when they get that look on their face like which one of us is really the human being and which one of us is the dog.

"And I look at him and I say, 'Himler. Out.' And he starts to growl. And I say, 'If you don't get out of that dog house I built for you, they'll be picking your brains up off the wet grass.'

"Now, Himler knows that when I am drinking I am not the gentle soul my wife is. So he sort of slowly slinks out in the rain. You know, whimpering. And I get down and squeeze myself into that dog house. Can you imagine? I mean can you really? I mean the thing smells of dog. He's got rags and bones and you name it in there. And I put my head on my wrists, just like a dog, and I try to go to sleep. But it takes me a while because Himler is whimpering."

— ✧ —

"What do you do to stay away from a drink?" Harry asked at the end of the meeting.

"I really don't have to do anything," Father Jim said. "There's no booze at Guest House."

Harry the Collector shook his head. "Don't they tell you to ask God to keep you away from a drink?"

"Yes. I guess so. Now that you mention it, they probably say that about ten times a day."

"But you don't do it? You're a priest and you don't pray?"

"Of course I pray," Father Jim said. His smile just barely hid his indignation.

Harry did not seem to notice or if he did, he did not care.

"When you pray, how do you pray?" he asked.

"I say Mass. I read the Divine Office every day. We have compline. Grace before meals. The rosary."

"Very impressive," Harry said. "Did all that stuff keep you away from alcohol?"

"What do you mean?" Jim asked.

"I mean, before you came out to Guest House, when you said Mass and did all that other stuff, did you stay away from a drink?"

"No," Jim said in a surprised tone. "I guess not."

"Are you doing anything different? Is there any reason why saying Mass and doing all that other stuff will keep you sober now?"

"Well," Jim thought, "I don't know. I guess not."

"Do you want to go back to the way you were before Guest House?"

"No," Jim said emphatically. "I do not."

"Well unless you learn how to pray the way we do in A.A. you don't have a chance of staying sober."

"Hey Jim, are you all set?" It was another of the priests.

Jim was staring at Harry and did not hear his name called.

"They want to go back, Father," Harry said. "I'll see you around."

"Wait a minute," Jim said to Harry. "Hang on for a minute or two," he said to the priest who called him. "You have to explain that to me. I mean, how do you pray in A.A."

"Are you going to the meeting tomorrow night?" Harry asked.

"Yes. I'll be there."

"We can talk then if you want to," Harry said.

— ✧ —

It was a mystery. How could a garbage collector know something about prayer that he didn't? Jim had read St. Teresa and John of the Cross. He had read *The Imitation of Christ* and *The Cloud of Unknowing*. He had read extensively about prayer. How could Harry know more about it than he did? And yet he seemed to. Jim spent most of the next day puzzling over it. It almost seemed that he was being unfaithful to the society. He was going to be instructed by a layman — not just a layman but a garbageman and a Protestant at that — in how to pray.

"Alcoholics are different," the doctor was saying. Some of the priests in the classroom took notes; others just listened. "There are times in the life of an alcoholic that he simply cannot resist the idea of a drink. He is powerless. If you reflect on it, you will probably see that there were times in your life when you drank when you didn't want to. Or that you drank at inappropriate times. You may not have given it much thought. You just drank.

"You know that most alcoholics at one time or another say that they will never drink again. Other people with allergies don't seem to have that problem. For example, somebody is allergic to penicillin. Goes into a coma. Almost dies. He will never have anything to do with penicillin again. He makes sure that if he goes into the hospital everybody knows that he cannot have penicillin. Why? Because it will kill him.

"Now, take the alcoholic. He goes into a coma and almost dies from drinking. Or he damages his liver to the point where drinking becomes a life-threatening proposition. And he gets out of the hospital and the first thing he wants to do is celebrate with a drink.

"That's insanity. Alcoholic insanity. But it is also powerlessness. There comes a time in the life of every alcoholic that no matter how much trouble alcohol has caused in his life, he simply has no defense against the first drink."

Jim nodded. It was true. He was the perfect example. Everything the doctor was talking about had happened to him. And when he got out of the hospital he drank. He was insane. He was powerless.

"It's a death sentence," he thought. "Alcoholism is a death sentence."

— ✧ —

Harry the Collector waved to him from across the room. Jim got a cup of coffee and went and stood with him.

"How's it going?" Harry asked.

"Bumpy, but it's going," Jim said.

"I was thinking about you on the route today," Harry said. "And I was wondering if you knew about being powerless."

"They talked about that today," Jim answered. "I think they probably talked about it before. But today when they talked about it, I realized they were talking about me. I mean, more than once I picked up a drink to celebrate getting out of the hospital after booze had put me in there in the first place. It is really unbelievable."

"Well, what are you going to do about it?" Harry asked.

"What do you mean?"

"Didn't they tell you that there will come a time when no power on Earth can keep you away from a drink?"

"Yes."

"Well?"

"Well, what?"

"Well, what are you going to do about it?"

"I don't know, "Jim said. "But I sure as hell don't want to drink."

Harry sighed. "Then you are going to get down on your knees, and ask a power greater than yourself to keep you away from a drink today. You are going to ask God to do for you what you can't do for yourself."

Jim looked surprised. "They've been telling me to do that right along."

"Have you been?"

"No," Jim said. "I didn't understand. I didn't think it was important."

"Waiting to understand things before you do them, will probably kill you," Harry the Collector said. "Take the suggestions. Do them. The understanding will come later."

Harry stood in silence for a moment, and then he added a post script.

"You're a Jesuit, right? You must have studied a lot of years. You probably know just about everything there is to know about stuff that you learn in universities. But what you got to realize now is that you don't know about the stuff that will keep you alive. Maybe the way you pray is good enough for most people. Maybe they don't need God to act in their lives the way you and I do. But your way of prayer isn't good enough to keep you sober. You got to ask for help, Father, or you're just not going to make it."

Early one morning, about a week later, Ripley bumped into Father Jim as the priest was on his way to the chapel.

"Father, you look a little brighter," Ripley said. "How are you feeling?"

"I had forgotten what it was like to be able to eat or to drink coffee without pain. It's amazing."

"And how's the back?"

"I guess I'm always going to have back pain. But it's a lot easier to live with since they got my stomach straightened out."

"That's wonderful. You look a lot happier, a little more sure of yourself."

"I've been asking for help, Rip. And it works. In fact, I'm on my way to do that now."

"You wait until you go to chapel in the morning before you ask for help?"

Jim felt like he had walked into a trap. "Of course I do," Jim said with emphasis. "I have always said my morning prayers in the chapel."

"Tell me, Father, did you ever pick up a drink on your way to the chapel?"

Jim thought for a moment. He remembered that when he was on vacation he had once passed out at 7 o'clock one Sunday morning on the floor of the sacristy of the church in his home town.

"Yes," he said meekly.

"Then first thing when you get out of bed in the morning, get down on your knees, and ask God to keep you away from a drink for today."

"I'll try, Rip. But I may forget."

"Father Jim," Ripley said, almost in the tone of a first sergeant, "when you go to bed tonight, stick one of your shoes way under the bed. Then when you get up you will have to get down on your knees to find it. While you're down there, ask for help."

Chapter Eight

"A couple of weeks ago, I was in downtown Detroit during the morning rush hour, and there were a lot of horns honking and traffic was backed up, so I knew something was going on. Being an old writer, my curiosity usually gets the best of me, and it did again this time, so I started walking down the street to see what was happening. The further I walked, the louder the horns got. Some drivers were standing in the street and others had their heads out their car windows to see what was going on. I walked faster and faster and the horns got louder and louder. People were swearing, and some of them were really enraged. Finally, I got down to a major intersection on Woodward Avenue. Traffic was backed up in all directions. And there, in the middle of the street, was a well-dressed fellow — who had obviously been drinking for a few days — directing traffic."

Ripley had warmed to his story. He paced back and forth across the front of the room as he spoke, and gestured widely with his arms to describe the chaos in the intersection.

"There was a young woman at the corner who stood watching all this, and she turned to me and said, 'That man is insane.' And I agreed. 'He sure is,' I said.

"Did anybody here ever direct traffic?" he asked. "I did. A couple of times. Why is it that drunks like to direct traffic? Anyway, I agreed with the woman that the man was insane. And the two cops who came and carted him off probably thought he was, too. But we thought he was insane for different reasons. The woman thought he was crazy because he was out in the middle of the morning rush hour directing traffic. Not me. I knew he was doing that because he was drunk not because he was insane."

Ripley stopped pacing.

"A lot of people get mixed up here. They think that alcoholic insanity is doing stupid things when you're drunk. That's not it at all. A non-alcoholic can get drunk and do something stupid, and the next morning when he wakes up, he can say, 'If that's what alcohol does to me, I'm not going to get drunk again.' And he won't. He sees the consequences of having too much alcohol, so he simply avoids having too much alcohol."

Ripley shook his head as if imagining the impossible, and the men in the room laughed.

"The alcoholic is not like that. We pick up a drink, get drunk and get in trouble. So we say, we'll never do that again. And then we pick up a drink, get drunk and get in trouble. And we say, 'Never again. This time it will be different.' So we pick up a drink, get drunk and get in trouble.

"One of the definitions of insanity is doing the same thing over and over but expecting different results. The results are ultimately always the same. If an alcoholic picks up a drink, sooner or later he will get in trouble. Period.

"But the alcoholic cannot grasp that simple fact. After a while when the idea of a drink comes into his mind, he cannot resist. He has no defense against it. His past troubles are forgotten. He only remembers the pleasurable feelings he has gotten from alcohol. So he says to himself, 'This time it will be different,' and he picks up a drink and three days later he ends up directing traffic during the morning rush hour.

"He's not insane because he directed traffic. He's insane because he picked up a drink. A sane man can look at an alcoholic and know that if he takes a drink he will continue to drink until he either passes out or there is no more booze available. But the alcoholic says to himself, 'This time it will be different.' And he believes it. That's insanity."

"I'm a failure as a priest. I'm a failure as a human being. I don't know how to pray. And on top of all that I'm insane," Jim said.

Ripley nodded his agreement.

"It's a challenge, isn't it," he said.

"A challenge?" Jim's tone was angry and incredulous.

"Yes."

"I'm fifty years old. I have to start my life all over. They're not going to want me back at the college. I'm a drunk. I've made a fool of myself. I'm a disgrace. Those bastards were right after all."

Ripley laughed.

"I don't see the humor in this," Jim said.

"Some day you will, Father Jim."

"Someday. Someday. Someday. I'm sick of someday. I'm sick of 'It will get better.' I'm sick of 'patience.' I'm sick of all that crap. What about now? That's what I want to know. What about now? I've been here since last fall. Am I going to have to spend the rest of my life in some godforsaken place in the middle of nowhere?"

"Getting a bit itchy?"

"A bit," Jim said, grudgingly, but then almost in spite of himself, the hint of a smile crossed his lips.

"Just when we think our life is over is when it truly begins," Ripley said.

"Do you really think so?" Jim asked.

"I've seen it a hundred times."

"I don't know, Rip. Sometimes I'm so full of shame. I don't know how I can ever face people. 'There's Jim Collins. The perfect example of what a Jesuit shouldn't be like.' "

Ripley laughed again.

"You laugh," Jim said. "But it's true. I can almost feel them pointing their fingers at me."

Ripley who had been leaning back in the swivel chair behind his desk now sat forward.

"Did you write out the second step as I suggested?" he asked.

"Yes."

"Do you have it with you?"

"No. But I remember what it said. 'We came to believe that a power greater than ourselves could restore us to sanity.' "

Ripley nodded. "We are powerless over alcohol and our lives are unmanageable. That's why we come here. We can't manage our own lives. We're out of control. And we are powerless to change that. But we come to believe that a power greater than ourselves can change us."

"I believe that," Jim said. "Theoretically."

"Theoretically?"

"I believe God can do anything He wants. He can even straighten my life out, if He wants to," Jim said.

"Jim", she said. "Get off the floor."

He opened his eyes and saw his mother standing over him. Old Father Riley was standing next to her. He was wearing his cassock and a black biretta — the three-cornered hat — and his arms were folded.

"Get this bum out of my sacristy," he said.

The words had echoed through Jim's head for days. "Get this bum out of my sacristy. Get this bum out of my sacristy."

He had agreed to say the seven o'clock Mass that Sunday. He did not remember getting to the church or getting vested. When he opened his eyes he was lying flat on his back, and he was wearing the vestments for Mass. An altar boy stood near the door. He must have gone to get the pastor when Jim collapsed or passed out. The boy, who was about ten years old, wore a red cassock and white surplus. He looked shocked.

His mother, on the other hand, just looked terribly wounded. Her hat was askew, and she looked as if she had dressed in haste. As she looked down at Jim her wounded look changed to a look of disgust.

"Get this bum out of my sacristy."

Jim looked at Ripley. "What a mess."

"What?" Ripley asked.

"My life. I look back sometimes and it looks like the scene of a hit-and-run accident. How could I go on like that? How could I do those things?"

"The wreckage of the past," Ripley said. "We all have it. I destroyed a marriage, ruined friendships."

"I can't imagine you doing those things," Jim said.

"We're survivors of a catastrophic disease," Ripley said. "We were possessed by alcohol. It had us, and there was no escaping."

His mother walked through the half open door and looked at the bed where Jim's suitcase lay open. Inside the suitcase there were two full quarts of Scotch and more than a half-dozen small bottles of pills. There were two kinds of sleeping pills and several types of tranquilizers and mood elevators.

"Is that a bar or a pharmacy?" his mother asked.

"Its all medicine mother. Some I drink and some I eat, but it's all medicine."

"Your brother is ready to take you to the train," she said. "I'll be right down. Before you go, I have something to say to you."

"That was an accident this morning, mom," Jim said. "That will never happen again."

"I don't want you to come home anymore," she said.

"What?"

"I don't want you to come home anymore."

"Mother."

"I can't live like this."

"It was an accident," Jim said.

"Not just this morning. Look at Friday night."

Jim turned to shut the suitcase.

"What about Friday night?" he asked.

"You don't remember?"
"Remember what?"

"I think you're almost ready, Father Jim," Ripley said.
"For what?"
"To take a long, hard look at the past. To look at it all — the good, the bad, the embarrassing, the achievements, the failures, the love, the lack of love — everything."
"The fourth step?"
Ripley nodded.
"I haven't done a third step yet," Jim said.
"I know."
"Shouldn't I do a third step first?"
"Yes. Did you write that out too?"
Jim nodded. "'We made a decision to turn our lives and wills over to the care of God, as we understand Him.'" he quoted. "But since I'm already a priest, do you think this is necessary?"
"Let's look at it for a moment."

He remembered that Friday only vaguely. He had taken the train to Boston and telephoned his mother from South Station.
"Were coming home for dinner," he said.
"Who's we?" his mother asked. There was concern in her voice.
"God and me," Jim said.
The Lone Ranger and Tonto, Jim thought. But which one was the Lone Ranger and which one was Tonto? Was God Tonto?

"First we realize that we are helpless against alcohol. And then we see God can keep us from a drink, and we come to believe that He can somehow mend our broken lives," Ripley said.

"The Lone Ranger and Tonto," Jim thought. "Me and God."

"And so we give Him our alcoholism. We give Him our present and our past and our future," Ripley said.

"Can He be trusted?" Jim thought. "What kind of thought is that? I'm a priest." He shifted in his seat. "But can He be trusted?" Jim thought.

"Self-will is the enemy," Ripley said. "Self-will and self-centeredness. Those are the destructive elements of our nature. If we don't get rid of them, or at least get them under control, they'll kill us."

"But what does God want?" Jim wondered. "Suppose I give Him my self-will and self-centeredness? What will He do? Will He let me go back to the college? Suppose His will is that I never get out of this place? Suppose His will is that I get run over by a bus?"

He had taken a cab from South Station to his house. The cab ride had cost more than the train fare. Later that night he telephoned a restaurant and had them deliver two full meals. Soup to nuts. Thirty-five dollars plus tip. His mother had paid, of course. He had taken the vow of poverty. He did not have any money.

"You only ate two forkfuls of that meal," she said. "Thirty-five dollars for two forkfuls."

"Mother, I'm sick. I'm not a well man."

*"Thirty-five dollars. I can't afford that. Thirty-five dollars
for you and God, and God didn't eat either."*
"That other meal was for you," he said.
"Well, I couldn't eat it. I was too upset."

"What do you think?" Ripley asked.

"It's a risk," Jim said.

Ripley smiled.

"I mean I don't know what His care for me is. It would
be easy if I knew what His care for me was going to be. But
I don't."

"Whatever His care is for you, Father Jim, remember
that it will be loving," Ripley said.

Jim shook his head.

"It's a risk. But I've got to give this mess to somebody,"
Jim said. "I can't straighten it out."

Ripley remained silent, looking across the desk at
Father Jim.

Finally, Jim spoke.

"I guess I've got to risk it," he said.

Chapter Nine

Something happened in Ripley's office that day, something that Jim was still undecided about. When the conversation was finished, the two men sat in silence for a long time. And then Jim had knelt down in front of Ripley's desk.

"Jesus," he had said aloud, "In your presence and in the presence of my friend Rip, I am making a decision to give everything to you. Everything in the past. My sins. My failures. My whole history. My sickness. My priesthood. Everything. And I give you the present. I give you my alcoholism and my recovery. I give you this day and everything in it. And I give you everything from this moment on. I give you my future life, my joys and my sorrows, and my life as a priest. And I thank you for your care, whatever that care is, even if it means getting hit by a bus. Amen."

"Amen," Ripley added.

When Jim got back to his feet, he had the strange sensation that there was another person in the room. He looked over his shoulder, but there was no one behind him. Still, he felt a presence. He looked at Ripley, but Ripley did not seem to be aware of anything unusual.

Later, alone in his room, he still felt a warmth, a tenderness that surrounded him and comforted him. He did not dwell on it mentally, instead, almost without paying attention to it or focusing on it, he luxuriated in it. He had a sense for the first time in many, many years that all was well and that all would be well.

He sat at his desk by the window looking out at the stark winter landscape, so forlorn in the dying light of the afternoon. In front of him was a loose-leaf binder that he purchased on one of his occasional forays to the village. On the first page he had written, "This is the Fourth Step Inventory of Rev. James D. Collins, S.J. Started Jan. 1, 1960."

He had begun a monumental task.

"Call it an autobiography," Ripley had said. "But it must be a fearless and searching moral inventory of yourself, and it has to be written down. Everything that is hidden must be revealed. All the good, all the bad, and all the inbetween. I found that for me, it was best to go over my whole life, from my first memory to the present, to take a look at everything in my past in terms of sex, society and security. There are lots of different ways of doing a Fourth Step, but an autobiography worked for me, and that's why I'm suggesting you do it that way, too."

Jim liked Ripley, and he admired his honesty, his moral energy, and his wisdom. Because of all that, he had asked Ripley to be his sponsor, a kind of spiritual director, advisor and wailing wall all rolled into one. And Ripley, after spelling out the ground rules, agreed. The ground rules pretty much boiled down to Father Jim agreeing to follow Ripley's suggestions.

He heard the sound of his own flesh searing on the stove. He screamed but he could not pull his hands away, they were stuck to burning hot cast iron. His mother spun around at the sink and stared at him, at first not registering what was happening. Then she sprang across the kitchen and ripped his hands from the stove. None of the other pain he had suffered in his life had ever matched that. He opened his hands and looked at his palms, still scarred after forty-five years. His mother had put some Vaseline on them, and he had been in agony for days. Since then, if he could avoid it, he never let anyone see the palms of his hands.

"Don't analyze it," Ripley said. "Just write it down. This isn't psychoanalysis, it's a fearless and searching moral inventory. And don't worry whether it is important or not, if it is still kicking around inside of you, write it down."

On the front door of the house on Cottage Street there was a huge bouquet with a purple ribbon.

His older brother Jack stood on the corner looking back at the house.

"Son of a bitch," Jack said. "Son of a bitch."

Jim stood next to him with his hands closed into fists. Occasionally, he would open one of his hands and examine his scarred palms and the silky smooth skin of his fingers.

"Son of a bitch," Jack said.

"Are we going in?" Jim asked.

They were both wearing dark suits and black ties, and each had a black ribbon tied around his upper left arm.

"Son of a bitch," Jack said.

People were already coming.

They were supposed to have been in the house a half-hour ago. Indeed, they had heard their mother calling them, but they had not answered.

"Are we going in?" Jim asked again.

"What I want to know is why. That's all. Why?" Jack said. "Somebody just tell me why."

"David J. Collins, Certified Public Accountant, Dies at Age 42. Serum Injection blamed." The paper lay open on the kitchen table.

Nobody was paying attention to it. The kitchen was mobbed. Just about everyone had a glass of whiskey in hand. There was laughter. There were even a few shouts.

Jim wandered through the dining room and into the living room. The casket was against the far wall. His father lay there, looking frozen and white, much older than he was, with a rosary wrapped around his chiseled hands.

His mother was to one side being consoled by a neighbor woman. Jim sat across the room from them observing everything. His father lay there, the almost unnoticed central figure. Indeed, Jim thought, he was already gone, already just a memory. He was suddenly unreachable. Jim turned to the wall so that no one could see the tears or hear his quiet sobs.

There was a knock at the door and Jim closed the loose-leaf binder.

"Come in," he said.

Fred entered with his overcoat over his arm.

"I'm just about to leave," he said.

"You're always way ahead of me," Jim said. "You got here first. You did your Fourth Step first, and now you're heading back to Massachusetts before me."

Fred managed a smile.

"Nervous?" Jim asked.

"I've been almost a year. Everybody here understands alcoholism."

"You'll be fine, Fred."

"I know. But I'm nervous anyway."

"You're a great friend, Fred."

Fred shifted his weight without responding.

"It took courage to tell me I was off base. You helped me a lot."

"You've helped me too, Jim."

"It's nice to know there will be a fellow sufferer at the Cross when I get back."

"Strength in numbers," Fred said.

The waves broke gently on the white sand. The sun was hot, massaging their bodies with its healing rays.

"Come on, Jimmy."

"Just call me the Bambino," Jim said, grabbing the sawed-off broom stick that they were using as a bat. "The King of Swat," he said, winking at Mary. He took a few practice swings and then got up to bat by a white towel they were using as home plate.

"Steee rike one," O'Leary shouted.

Jim raised his hand like Casey at the Bat to still the turbulent mob.

"Stee rike two," O'Leary screamed.

Jim stepped out of the batter's box and looked at the ocean. Then he used the bat to point out to sea. That was where he intended to hit the next pitch.

His brother Jack went into an elaborate windup and fired the rubber ball toward the target the crouching O'Leary made with his hands.

Jim swung from his heels using every ounce of muscle in his body. He simultaneously missed the ball and heard the short cracking sound in his back. He collapsed in pain.

Everybody thought he was joking.

"The Great Bambino strikes out," O'Leary shouted.

Even Mary, who had an overwhelming crush on Jim, stood smiling as he lay on the sand rocking and grimacing in pain.

Since he took that mighty swing on the beach more than thirty years earlier, he had never experienced one day without pain. Some days were worse than others, but always there was pain.

Shadowbrook, Keyser Island, Guest House. "I have spent a lot of my life in mansions," Jim wrote. "It's like living in an expensive tent."

Shadowbrook was an estate in the Berkshires built by Andrew Carnegie, but later acquired by the Society. He had lived there as a novice. It was a spartan life. He thought it was probably tougher than being a Marine recruit.

But Jim had accepted the life without question. The estate was isolated — nine miles from Pittsfield — and the novices were isolated. They were not allowed to see newspapers or listen to the radio. He had entered Shadowbrook in September of 1929 but he did not hear about the stock market crash until Christmas. Even then, he was removed from it, unaffected by it and by the world.

As he looked back on those days, what he remembered most were the bells, which regulated his life and movements, and the cold. The novices slept in dormitories, and some nights it was almost impossible to get warm, no matter how many blankets were piled on top of the bed. And there were the cold water shaves at five in the morning, and the mandatory outdoor exercise, no matter what the weather conditions.

There were the subtle safeguards which he hardly noticed. When novices went for a walk, there had to be three of them. There was a rule against touching.

And there was the beauty of nature, the magnificence of the Berkshires, pines and birches, gray stone walls wandering through woodlands, and the rivers, ponds and bracing air.

They were hardy men. They studied hard and they worked hard. And most of them were athletes. They played football and ice hockey with a special ferocity, and they loved to climb mountains and canoe down rivers.

They had a sense of being special. They were in training to be soldiers of Christ — the Pope's very own.

Jim was at Weston studying philosophy when Prohibition was repealed. When he walked into the dining room there was a buzzing and a laughter that he usually associated with holidays. On a table, near the kitchen was a gallon jug of port wine and students and teachers were bunched together talking and joking. Before he could ask, someone handed him a glass.

It was one of the most pleasant experiences of his life. The camaraderie, the warmth, the acceptance. It was fun. It only lasted a half an hour, but the memory of the conversation and the friendship stayed with him. He had loved it. He had loved the conversation and the relaxation, and he had loved the sharp taste of the port, and the warm feeling it spread through him when it hit the bottom of his stomach.

There was something else that happened during those thirty minutes — he was free from physical pain for the first time in almost ten years, and all the inner anxiety, and the nervousness and the self-doubt disappeared. Suddenly he had felt like the Bambino. He felt like a major leaguer, but not just any major leaguer, but the Bambino himself. Jim Collins was the Babe Ruth of the dining hall.

"Learning anything?" Ripley asked.

"I'm getting a much different picture of me," Jim answered. "There are some contradictory things. I always thought I was a joyous person, but as I look back, I've had some pain. I never realized how devastated I was by my father's death or how ashamed I was that I damn near burnt all the skin off my hands and my mother never took me to the doctor. Even now I don't want people to see the palms of my hands. It's like I don't want them to see my imperfections. Father Jim is supposed to be the perfect human being. If they see one defect, they might realize I'm full of them."

"Sounds like you're making progress."

"There's something else, Rip. I haven't written it down yet, but it's sort of in the background of everything I've looked at."

Ripley nodded, almost as if he knew what Jim was going to say.

"It's a tough admission for a Jesuit," Jim said. "But I guess it was a question I was afraid to ask myself. But it was always there, always sort of nagging at me. I always wondered if God loved me. Here I was doing all this stuff for Him, but I wondered if it mattered to Him. He seemed to ignore me. He seemed to ignore my pain. I guess I suspected that He had turned His back on me, but I was afraid to even think it."

The two men were near the front door. Jim had just returned from a meeting and he was still wearing his overcoat. Ripley looked as if he had just taken a shower and put on a clean set of clothes. His starched blue shirt was perfectly smooth, and his bald head gleamed with the reflected light of the hall chandelier.

"There's one other thing. Sort of strange. Maybe you'll think I'm nuts. But since I took the Third Step in your office, I've had the sensation — that of a presence — I mean, right here. It's like someone walking along next to me with an arm around my shoulder.

"It's as if He's saying, 'It's okay, Jim. It's all right. It's all downhill from here.' "

Chapter Ten

$\mathcal{I}$ don't know what came first — the hunger or the pain. I wanted to be. There was this great yearning within me. I wanted people to stop what they were doing and say, 'There goes Jim Collins — a hell of a guy. Full of life, full of fun, full of wisdom.'

(Father Jim, can you teach me to drink like you do?)

First class. That's why the Jesuits attracted me — a first class outfit.

— Jim, that's the most expensive tennis racket in the store.

— I know, Dad. (I called him Dad. It had not been easy when my mother married again. But he was a nice guy.) But the weight is right and the balance is really good. (I loaned it to the kid on the tennis team — what was his name? — and I never saw it again. I only used it once or twice.)

First Class Collins, they could have called me. It is all so convoluted — the good times and the bad times. I used to tend bar at some of the functions.

— Father Jim, where did you learn to make a martini?

— There was a special course in my juniorate.

— You're amazing. I wish I could drink like you. You never seem to show any effects.

— It's a gift. It's only given to a chosen few. It's called tolerance. I have a high degree of tolerance.

Every so often, I would get a whiff of perfume, or an attractive woman would touch my hand and look earnestly into my eyes, and I could feel my whole being radiate towards her. It would be more than sexual, more than that nagging sense of never being complete, it would be as if a whole dimension of my life was sealed off, as if there was a beautiful room that I was not allowed to enter or to know about.

— Don't dwell on it Jim. The thoughts come to us all. We're men. Our sexuality is God-given. But he also gives us the power to channel that energy into other things, to use it in many productive ways.

Did I know what I was giving up when I gave it up? Somebody asked me that once — an alumnus back for homecoming — we were sitting in the autumn twilight with drinks in our hands staring down at the city.

— Did you know what you were giving up? Or were you too young? I thought about it. The decision just seemed to happen. I was at the college. All men. All Catholic. Jesuits were larger than life. They were manly and athletic. I used to pass the word that my brother Jack was interested in joining up, and they would come into the room and talk to him. I would sit there almost unnoticed and listen. Jack thought it was a great joke. He always went along with it. Never complained.

— Did you know what you were giving up, Father? Love, children, a career?

I could hear the orchestra playing inside. The alumni and their wives were dancing. I did not know what I was giving up. Even at that moment, I did not know what I had given up. How could I? I had never really held a woman in my arms. I had never had a son to follow me around. The drink softened the

*question. It made everything theoretical. There was no hunger,
no lost dimension.*

*— Did you know what you were giving up when you got
married? I asked him.*

Fred was much more systematic than Jim. He had
begun at the beginning and worked his way through. Jim
could not do that. He was sporadic and haphazard. He
could not stay with a train of thought for too long.

"Don't worry about it. You're not out to win a Pulitzer
Prize for biography. Keep writing. And after a while all
these seemingly random thoughts will turn out to be like
tiles in a mosaic, and at some point you will begin to see
the whole picture," Ripley told him.

Jim sighed. He did not like the discipline of writing
every day. It seemed like a task he would never finish.

"And you really think it's that important?"

"It's a matter of life and death," Ripley said.

"Just writing all this stuff down?"

"Life and death, Father Jim."

*That's what the nembutal had seemed like — a matter of
life and death. Jack had prescribed it. At first it had seemed like
a miracle drug. The back pain disappeared. I slept like a baby.
I woke up refreshed. I was a new man.*

*An end of pain, an end of the raw nagging that was always
at the boundary of my consciousness. Scraggy Collins.*

Who used to call me that? Scraggy.

*That's when I started to wear two cassocks with a heavy
sweater underneath so no one could tell how thin I was.*

And some of them would still say — Here comes Scraggy.

It was a joke. It was just in fun. But it hurt.

I used to wonder what they would call me if they found out I was wearing a ton of clothes.

Or did they know?

When you live in a close community, people always know more than you think they know. They give you that look, like —
What have you been into?

Like my mother when she saw the suitcase full of booze and pills on the bed.

— What have you been into this time, Jim?

As if I was five or six years old.

— What have you been into?

I was into all kinds of drugs and I didn't realize it. I really didn't realize it. I was addicted and I didn't know it. How is that possible? How can you be addicted to drugs and not know it? How can you be an alcoholic and not know it?

I can still see Doctor Brophy standing in the hospital room trying to tell me I was a drunk, and he couldn't do it, and I wouldn't have believed him anyway. How is that possible? How can you be so sick and not know it's the booze?

I was like the cuckold. I was the last to know.

No wonder they were so frustrated with me. They knew what my problem was, and they must have thought that I knew what my problem was.

— Come on, Jim, Bill Donahue had said more than once. Come on, Jim, we both know what's going on.

— Do you? I used to think. Do you? I've got pain that goes right into my soul. I have a chilling fear that paralyzes me. You don't know. Nobody has any idea. I don't even think God knows.

— Come on, Jim. This has been going on far too long.

— For Christ's sake, I thought. For Christ's sake.

— Far too long, Jim. Far too long.

— For the sake of Christ.

— ✧ —

Spring came to Lake Orion as a surprise. One day there were snow flurries, the next was sunny and warm with swelling buds and birds calling to each other. Jim was less of a stick man than he had been in years. He weighed more than one hundred twenty pounds, and the gaunt look had left his face. He began to spend more and more time outside, bundled up more than the other men, and usually walking alone. Other priests had come to Guest House, stayed for a few months and left, but Jim remained. Bill Donahue told Ripley that Jim could take whatever time was needed.

"Life is quieter here," Father Donahue said. "Fred seems to be very busy. He's always running out to a meeting. And strange people come on to the campus to pick him up or drop him off. But he hasn't had a drink, and that's a blessing."

"No problem with the bishop?" Ripley asked.

"None at all. He seems to understand this thing better than the rest of us. He said that he had no objection to Fred going to meetings wearing his collar and that Jim can too when he comes back."

"Speaking of Jim," Father Donahue continued, "He has not had a drink in seven months?"

"That's right."

"But you're cloistered."

"Not at all," Ripley said.

"Seven months," Father Donahue repeated. "It's been pretty quiet around here."

"Sanity has returned to Holy Cross."

"Yes. It's been pretty sane around here without Jim."

——◆——

Sometimes there were two sides to me that were quite oppo-site and quite extreme. I think now that they were always there, but they didn't really become pronounced until long after I had become a Jesuit.

I always wanted the best of everything. Top shelf. Whiskey or clothes. Even my black suits were expensive. There were always gifts. Some rich alumnus always wanted to shell out money. I loved good shoes. I liked the dignity of good tailoring. And they would tell me to go to an exclusive men's store and charge it to their account, and I would.

And as long as I can remember, I have always liked to take taxis.

— Where to, Father?

— Oh, lets just drive around for a while and see what's hap-pening in the city.

They never complained about the bills from the cab company. Never even asked about them. There was something about get-ting out of a cab downtown and handing the driver a tip (I always charged the ride to the college but handed the driver a healthy tip) that made me feel good.

— Jim, I simply can't afford this kind of extravagance.

— Oh, mother.

— Other people take the bus.

— Other people are not Jesuits.

"I would rather be judged by Jesus Christ than by my moth-er," our founder said. I think I agree with him.

How did she put up with me for so long?

So, there was the grandiosity. Tailored suits, cabs, filet mignon and the race track. Yes, the race track. I loved the track. I probably still do. Sometimes I thought the horses ran just for me.

First Class Collins. Top shelf. Scraggy.

Grandiosity. And beneath it the sense that I was displeasing to God, to the Society, to just about everybody.

Finally, I stopped saying Mass. Nobody told me to. I just did. I felt my very presence on the altar was a sacrilege.
  — *Do priests go to confession, or do they just forgive themselves?*
  — *Of course we go to confession.*
  — *Suppose a priest commits a mortal sin and doesn't have time to go to confession before he's supposed to say Sunday Mass? What does he do?*
  Students love to ask questions like that. Some of the questions are bizarre.
  — *Would you ever kiss a leper like St. Francis did?*
  — *Only Franciscans kiss lepers.*
  — *Can you imagine kissing somebody's open wound? Why did he do that?*
  Why indeed? Francis always troubled me. He was like a personal accusation. He never went to the track. He never ate filet mignon. He got rid of all his fancy clothes. Stripped right in the center of town. Can you imagine that? Standing naked in the middle of town? And kissed the leper.

— ✧ —

There was hunger and pain. There was grandiosity and the certain knowledge that I was not worthy to be a priest.
  Domine, non sum dignus, ut intres sub tectum meam: sed tantum dic verbo. et sanabitur anima mea.
  That is why I stopped saying Mass. I was not worthy, and I did not believe he would say the word. My soul could not be healed.
  What do you do if you're a priest and you are not worthy? What do you do if you are a bad priest? A disgrace?
  I drank.
  Which came first the bad priest or the drink?

— ✧ —

"I want you to list your good qualities," Ripley said.

Jim smiled almost ruefully.

"That's grandiosity in reverse," Ripley said.

"What is?"

"Denying that you have any good qualities."

Some of the old Jesuits were saints. I knew that. I could see it in their faces. They had a quality of goodness, of wisdom, of peace.

Beneath the grandiosity there was that hunger. I wanted to do something worthwhile, something noble. I wanted to touch hearts, to enlighten. I wanted to be a blessing in the lives of others.

What happened?

Pills. Booze. It was all so gradual. I didn't set out to drink. I didn't set out to become addicted to drugs. Pain, pills, booze. Pain, pills, booze. More and more. I forgot about being a blessing in the lives of others. I was simply First Class Collins.

But there was more to it than that. Deep down, very deep, very far down, I still had the hunger. I still wanted to serve. I still wanted to kiss the leper.

But I couldn't. Booze, pills, and pain.

We sat on the wall on Keyser Island staring out at the Sound.

— It's God that's doing this to us, Fred said.

Fred is steady, when he's not drinking. Sometimes he is profound. You don't think so because he is so quiet and withdrawn. He's like one of those civil servants in czarist Russia that never gets a promotion.

— *It's God that's doing this to us.*

It was like an echo.

Behind it all was the hand of God.

— *We must learn to see the hand of God behind the slap in the face.*

Who said that?

Fred would know.

The loving hand of God behind the slap in the face.

Fred loves paradoxes.

I'm not crazy about them. I don't like slaps in the face.

— *It's God that's doing this to us, Jim.*

I see two pictures. In one, there is a healthy, happy man standing straight up with a smile beaming from his face. He seems athletic and very intelligent. He looks younger than he really is. People naturally take to him. They like his company. They love to hear him speak.

In the other, there is a man in a wrinkled suit, bent over in pain. He walks with a cane and he longs for sleep, perhaps he longs to die. No one wants to come near him. He is like a plague.

I am the person in both pictures.

How do you account for that?

— *Its God that's doing this to us, Jim.*

Chapter Eleven

It was a little like taking off all of your clothes in the town square. And it was very draining. Father Jim and Ripley had been in Ripley's office for more than three hours as page by page and incident by incident, Jim had revealed the contents of his own searching moral inventory. He told Ripley about every embarrassing episode in his life, he told him of his secret sins, and he told him of his longings. Through it all, Ripley was silent and impassive. Once in a great while, Ripley would nod in agreement or in understanding. It was the only indication Jim had that he was listening.

"Well, what do you think?" Ripley asked when Jim was finished.

"I've made general confessions, I've done the Spiritual Exercises, but I've never experienced anything like this," Jim said.

"In what way?"

"I've seen things I've never seen before. I have a new understanding of myself."

Ripley smiled.

"I'm sick. I don't mean my back or my stomach. I mean that something within me is broken. I didn't choose to screw up my life. I wanted to be a good priest, a good teacher. Alcoholism took that away from me. Once I got into the booze I was a goner. I couldn't do what I wanted to do. And after a while I forgot what I wanted to do. Booze called the shots. I was like a marionette and booze was pulling the strings. What a waste.

"And that's not all. On top of that, I can see this incredible self-centeredness. For the last twenty or thirty years, the only person I have been concerned about is me. My mother must have gone through terrible torment when she had to come down and pick me off the sacristy floor and take me home. But I didn't give her a thought. It never occurred to me that I put the men I live with through hell. I was right. They were wrong. They simply didn't understand."

Ripley stretched back in his chair and examined the ceiling above Jim's head.

"It's a tough job, telling somebody all about yourself. You've done it admirably, fearlessly. You have shed light on all the dark corners. And I have not rejected you," Ripley said.

Jim looked surprised.

"Was there a danger of that?" he asked.

"No," Ripley replied.

"But you knew that I was afraid that you might reject me?"

"Yes."

Jim thought for a moment.

"And when you did your fifth step with your sponsor, you were afraid he might reject you."

"That's right," Ripley said.

"But he didn't."

"Right again."

That night, Jim was exhausted. It was a bone weariness. He felt as if he had been through a tremendous ordeal, and he felt that he had emerged victorious, but he was too tired to celebrate. He lay on his bed. His mind was empty. There were no errant thoughts buzzing around. He was utterly depleted.

Gradually, despite his tiredness, a feeling of joy began to fill him. He had done it the way it was suggested. He had been honest, fearless and searching. He had looked at himself without blinking and without covering anything up. He had told Ripley everything. There were no more secrets. He had come a long way from the hospital and from the college. He had come a long way from his last drink. He had a newfound knowledge. He wasn't much of a priest. He wasn't much of a man. He was self-centered and grandiose. He was burdened by his own defective character and by a powerful and deceitful disease. But now he knew it. At last he knew it. Finally, he knew what was wrong with him.

There was a knock at the door. When there was no answer it was opened slightly. Another priest looked in. Jim was lying on the bed sound asleep.

"I guess Jim doesn't want to go to a meeting tonight," the priest said.

After a few weeks, Jim began to feel like an old-timer, and, indeed, he had been at Guest House longer than any of the other priests. They came to him for advice and for comfort. Sometimes he felt very wise. Sometimes he felt like a bishop.

"The Fifth Step is a beginning, not the end," Ripley told him. "You have simply discovered the defective nature of your character. Knowing about your defects doesn't mean they will go away by themselves."

Jim was stung. He did not let Ripley see it, but he was stung.

He was almost fifty-one years old. He was sober. And he was a Jesuit. Other priests were coming to him for help.

"This is not the real world. This is a haven — a place out of the storm. Sobriety must be lived out there in the hurricanes of life where people don't understand alcoholism. And if we let our character defects go untended they will kill us. They are lethal. You never know which one will kill you."

Ripley's words seemed rather dramatic.

"Kill me?" Jim asked.

"That's right. You have a fatal disease. It is your character defects which will lead you to pick up a drink. Grandiosity, self-centeredness, self-pity. And if you pick up a drink it will kill you. If you stay sober, you'll see it happen a thousand times. People get sober. They get a new lease on life. But they don't do anything to change. They hang on to their character defects as if they were gold. And sooner or later they pick up a drink, and then you read about them in the paper. You see them on the obituary page or you read about them in the court news. Their livers give out or they shoot themselves, or they run somebody over, or they're arrested for embezzlement. It happens all the time. People get the opportunity to change their lives, but they don't want to face themselves. Humility is the price of sobriety."

Jim nodded as if in agreement, but it stung. Ripley had seen right through him. He wasn't a wise man — he wasn't a bishop, Ripley seemed to be saying. He was just a drunk who had been sober for a short time.

"God damn it," Jim said angrily. "Grandiosity."

Ripley laughed.

Jim looked crestfallen.

"I'm grandiose. And on top of that I swear," Jim said.

Ripley laughed again.

"This disease would make a saint swear," he said.

Itchy.

It was the way he used to feel a day or two before he got out of the hospital, and it was the way he felt now.

Guest House was fine up to a point. But it had lost some of its attraction when Ripley reminded him that he was not an exemplar, that he was just another alcoholic priest trying to stay sober.

He was also getting a little bored with the A.A. meetings. A lot of the same people seemed to be saying the same things. And some of them seemed too happy to be real.

And there was the garbageman, the one who had instructed him about praying.

What would his fellow priests think about that? What would the students back at the college think, if he should inform them during a theology class that he had been taught how to pray by a garbage man?

And on top of that he was getting sick of the food.

As usual Ripley was resplendent in his attire. The warm rays of the sun bounced off his bald head. As friendly as he was, he seemed remote to Father Jim, as if he was already something out of the past.

"This has been quite an experience," Jim said.

"Hang on to it," Ripley said. "When you get back to the college start going to meetings from the first day. Father Fred is already quite involved in A.A. there. So it shouldn't be too difficult."

They shook hands.

"Write to me and let me know how you're doing," Ripley said. Then he pulled the priest towards him and gave him a bear hug.

It brought him back to his first meeting with Ripley, and Father Jim felt himself on the verge of tears.

"Mixed emotions," Ripley said.

Jim thought about Ripley as he rode to the airport. The man frequently seemed to know what he was thinking. Did he know that Jim had felt wounded when his lingering grandiosity was pointed out to him? Did he know that Jim both admired and resented him?

The driver took Jim's suitcase to the ticket counter and then offered the priest his hand.

"Good-bye Father Jim. I hope we'll meet again some day."

It was the same man who had driven him out to Guest House on his arrival almost a year earlier.

Jim reached in his pocket and handed the man five dollars.

The man seemed surprised.

"You don't have to do that Father. I'm just another guy trying to stay sober."

"It's all right," Father Jim said. "It makes me feel good."

The two men laughed.

PART TWO

Kissing the Leper

Chapter One

Holy Cross had not changed. Stately trees lined the drive past the library and up to Fenwick Hall which had been the first building Jim had entered when he came to the college as a student thirty-three years earlier. Below the college lay Worcester, an amalgam of blue-collar workers and their educated children. It was a city with a split personality, grime and brilliance stood side by side and each took a bit from the other. It was a city where education was both honored and despised. It was a city which prided itself on being a melting pot, but a city where ethnic divisions remained strong. There were Yankees, Irish, French, Italian, Lithuanian, Polish and Jews. And each ethnic group prided itself on being a little better than the others, but each felt, at the same time, defensive and alone.

The college sat on a hill to the windward side of the city. Immediately below it were factories and cramped tenements called three-deckers. The neighborhoods were dotted with bars and the bars were dotted with salt shakers. It was the custom to serve draft beer without a head so that the glass would be filled to the brim. Then after the patron sipped some beer off the top he would sprinkle salt in the glass to give the beer a head. In many ways it was a tough city where the old guard did its best to keep the newer ethnic groups suppressed. To the old guard unions were anathema. They ended the paternalism and autocratic rule of the rich. So the old guard despised unions and those who joined them, not because unions reduced their profits, but because the unions reduced their power to manipulate the ethnic groups. The old guard tended to see themselves as the elite, the chosen, and to see the ethnic groups as people who had been ordained to serve them faithfully, quietly and wholeheartedly. To the old line, keeping wages down was part of a holy war because if everyone had money and everyone could afford all the material benefits in life, then everyone would be part of the elite, and they would no longer be special.

One of the things that Jim liked about Holy Cross was that it was insulated from the city. The ethnic divisions were severely reduced on the hill. All of the students were male, almost all of them were Catholics, and most of them were Irish. There were, of course, Italians and French, Lithuanians and Poles, there was even an occasional Negro, but primarily, the college was Irish Catholic. The students were mostly from families who went to Mass on Sunday and voted Democratic. They were young, eager and clean cut. Many would go on to make major contributions in government and the professions. And they would base their lives on principles that they had learned at the college from Jim and men like Jim.

Jim had always loved the Catholic ideal. He had loved the thought of contributing to the education of young Catholic men. He had loved being a part of the college. But as the taxi pulled up in front of Fenwick, he wanted to slink down in the seat and tell the driver to drive him back to the city. He did not want to face the accusing eyes of his fellow Jesuits. The last time he was on the campus, he had been in disgrace as he had been many times before.

"Get this bum out of my sacristy," the old pastor in his hometown had said.

"Get this bum off our campus," Jim was sure that many of the Jesuits had thought and perhaps said to each other.

Bill Donahue was walking from the Hall to the library and stopped at the cab.

"Hello, Jim," he said, as Jim struggled to get out.

"Hi, Bill," Jim answered. He looked in Father Donahue's eyes and saw the unspoken question.

"Welcome home," Bill Donahue said. But the question was still there, and they both knew it.

"Thanks," Jim said. "It's good to be back."

Fred had waited all day for Jim to appear. He knew that he was back on campus, but Jim had apparently gone straight from the taxicab to his room and had not been seen since. Around two o'clock, Fred had knocked on the door to Jim's room, but there was no answer. So at about five o'clock, Fred went to the priest's dining room and camped out. It was not until almost seven, when most of the priests had already eaten and left, that Jim came in. He went to the counter and filled about half of his plate with food. Then, looking around the room, he saw Fred in a far corner, and only because it was impolite for a man to eat by himself, he made his way to Fred's table.

"You're back," Fred said.

"Yeah. Ain't life grand."

"I'm going to a meeting in about an hour. Want to come?"

"Not tonight. I'm tired. Long trip," Jim said.

"It will do you good," Fred persisted.

"I need my rest."

"Okay," Fred said. "There's another meeting tomorrow night."

"I'll have to see how I feel," Jim said.

Fred started to speak but stopped himself. He got up from the table and left the room without saying another word.

The drama built for three days in the Jesuit community. Jim kept to himself as much as possible while the other priests waited. Father Donahue called Fred into his office.

"What can we do?" he asked.

"Pray," Fred said.

"Is that all?"

"That's all," Fred said. "No human being can force another person to stay sober. The only one who can keep Jim sober is God. But even God can't keep him sober if Jim doesn't cooperate."

"Should I talk to him?"

"God?" Fred asked. And then the tension in the room broke as both men laughed.

"If you talk to Jim, it could backfire."

"You mean, he could get mad and go out and get drunk."

"Yes," Fred answered.

"This is like sitting on a keg of dynamite," Father Donahue said.

"Think how Jim feels," Fred said.

Bill Donahue looked surprised as if Jim's feelings were the last thing on his mind.

— ✧ —

"They think I'm some kind of cripple," Jim said.

"I guess they do," Fred said. "They think I am too."

"Like we're subhumans."

"That may be the way they think," Fred said.

"I don't like it."

"You don't have to like it," Fred said. "I don't like it either. But I'm not going to drink over it."

"Neither am I," Jim said.

"Really?"

Jim looked at Fred angrily.

"What is that supposed to mean?"

"It means you don't know which character defect is going to get you drunk."

This time, Jim did not respond.

"The battle is not between you and them," Fred said. "The battle is between you and your self-will. And there is no possible way you can win that battle alone."

Fred waited for his words to sink in.

"I'm going to a meeting tonight. Do you want to come?" Fred asked.

"That's like admitting to these bastards that I'm a cripple."

"So what?"

Jim did not have an answer.

"Let me think about it," he said.

But when Fred came back to Jim's room at seven that night, Jim was not there. Fred scoured the campus, but he could not find Jim.

The drama grew, and Fred became more and more fearful for his friend and for himself. Because if Jim drank after almost a year at Guest House, who was to say that Fred could stay sober?

The Arnold Street meeting was on the third floor of an old downtown building. The first floor housed a bar. The second floor was vacant. There was no sign indicating where the Alcoholics Anonymous meeting was. And people who wanted to attend the meeting entered a murky hall filled with the smell of urine and stale cigarette butts. At that point, some decided against A.A. and went to the bar on the first floor. Others climbed the badly lighted stairs to the third floor and knocked on the unmarked door.

Arnold Street had been the first meeting Fred had gone to when he returned from Guest House. He had gone dressed in his black suit with his Roman collar, and when he addressed the meeting he had given his full name and his telephone number. Some of the members were shocked. They didn't like last names. They didn't want the outside world to know where they were and who they were. Anonymity was a cloak of safety. Fred had threatened their safety, and they told him so. Fred had been contrite. He had also been faithful. He was constantly attending meetings, and he proved to be humble and willing to listen. He was also very nervous and his head would frequently wag from side to side. But despite his nervousness and shyness, people liked him and it did not take long for the members to realize that he was a man in hot pursuit of sobriety.

As he climbed the stairs, Fred did not feel as though he was in hot pursuit of anything. He was scared and depressed. He was sure that Jim had left the campus to drink, and he could already feel the consternation of his fellow Jesuits, and he could already feel that they were waiting for him to follow Jim's example. And Fred was terrified that he might do that. After all, did he really have any defense against alcohol or was it just a mirage? The stench of the stairwell was overpowering. In the room on the third floor there was just a collection of drunks. There were no psychiatrists or psychologists. There were just drunks, and some of them had had a drink on the way up the stairs. Sobriety was so flimsy. And A.A. didn't seem too substantial either. Rented quarters in a rundown building. No hospitals. No professionals. Just a bunch of drunks meeting in ugly rooms, drinking coffee and talking to each other. It was almost laughable. How could that help people? How could it keep them from slipping over the edge of insanity? It didn't make any sense. Indeed, it seemed utter foolishness for a theologian, who had studied for ten years before he became a priest, to get involved with a bunch of winos who had never heard of Thomas Aquinas or William of Ocham.

By the time Fred reached the third floor, he was ready to turn around and go home. He stood at the door, but he did not knock, debating with himself whether to go in or to go back down the stairs. He could not make up his mind, and he seemed to be frozen to the spot where he stood. But gradually, he decided that he was too tired to go to a meeting, too frustrated, too depressed, that what he needed was some time by himself, alone in his room, where he could think, where he could get it all sorted out.

He was about to start back down the stairs when the door opened and a woman in her late forties named Eleanor stepped into the hallway and touched Fred on the arm.

"Father, I thought someone was out here. It's good to see you. Are you coming in?"

Fred hesitated. "I guess so," he said.

There were about twenty-five people in the smoke-filled room, and every one of them held a paper cup filled with coffee. As Fred drifted toward the table with the coffee urn, he saw someone approach him out of the corner of his eye.

He turned and there was Jim with a huge beaming smile.

"Hi, I'm Father Jim, and I'm an alcoholic," Jim said, offering his hand to Fred.

The tension went out of Fred's face, but he did not smile as he shook Jim's hand.

"Thank God for that," he said.

Chapter Two

They were quite a collection: doctors, salesmen, lawyers, bums, whores, housewives, and priests. Almost all of them smoked rather furiously, and every one of them drank coffee. They gathered in the meeting room on the third floor of Arnold Street like fugitives from a storm. But they were happy fugitives, and sometimes the noise level reached such a crescendo that a passerby might have attributed the sounds he heard to a drunken brawl. The laughter often rolled out in high-pitched shrieks, and occasionally in the tones of a basso profundo. There were a lot of men named John in the room, and since members did not use last names, they picked up nicknames in order to distinguish them. There was John the Indian, John the electrician, John with whiskers, John the marine, and a man called

Possum, whose real name was John. There was even Big John and Little John.

There were people in the room who had not had a drink in twenty years and there were people in the room who had not had a drink in twenty minutes. And the discerning could tell which were which just by looking into their eyes. The booze-breathed arrivals tended to hunch their shoulders and avert their eyes. Their hands quivered as they tried to sip coffee. Some of them came because they wanted to try it, wanted to see if they could break the cycle of drinking. Some of them came because they were forced to. Some of them came once and never returned. Some of them came once and stayed for a lifetime.

Harry the Russian kept score. He would diligently record the name of each newcomer, and then in booming earnestness he would tell them, "It's a fatal disease. You don't do something for it, you die. Simple. But fatal. Simple but fatal."

Much of what Harry said was lost in his accent. He spoke fast and cared little for syntax or pronunciation. But his message that alcoholism was a fatal disease almost always came through. Frequently, he would reach into his pockets and pull out newspaper clippings from the obituary pages.

"See. She vas here two weeks. She don't come back. She die."

Harry would shake his head and fix his listener with his eyes.

"Him?" he asked pointing to another clipping. "Rope over plumbing."

"What?" the newcomer would ask.

"You know. Hang rope from pipe. Jump from chair. Dead. No more meetings."

"Oh, a suicide."

"A suicide," Harry agreed solemnly. "And this one sleep on tracks. Lots of drunks sleep on tracks. Why? Who knows?"

By this time the newcomer would be looking for a way of escape.

"Since I first come, one hundred twenty-six people die. Maybe you be one hundred twenty-seven. Who knows? Possibility. You may stick, get sober. Who knows? Grace of God. What's your name?"

"What do you want my name for?"

"I keep track. Helps me be sober."

Harry was something of a miracle. He had been a derelict who begged or did odd jobs to get money for wine. He slept in doorways when it was cold and in the tall grass when it was not. He had been known as a raucous drunk who loved to dance and declaim in a deep-throated and forceful Russian, and he cared nothing at all that his listeners could not understand him. He was often picked up by the police, but he never caused trouble so they almost always let him go without a court appearance. Four years before Fred and Jim arrived on the scene, people in the bar on Arnold Street wanted to get rid of Harry, so they told him there was free wine upstairs at the A.A. meeting. Harry had never heard of A.A. so he went upstairs looking for wine. The people took him in and treated him like one of their own. And instead of finding wine, Harry found sobriety.

The majordomo of Arnold Street was a man called Ernie G. He was a newspaper reporter who had almost drunk himself to death on the police beat eighteen years earlier. Indeed, his toe had been tagged at the city hospital because his alcoholic coma was at first thought to be death.

When he came to, after three days, a doctor and a man named Charlie were standing next to his bed. They told him that they were alcoholics and that he was one too. They said that they had found a way out and if he was interested they would share it with him. Even in the haze, Ernie was interested. When he got out of the hospital, he joined the other two men, and for a while, the three of them made up the entire fellowship of A.A. in the city. But they were not content with that. So they bailed out drunks, they visited hospitals, and they went on house calls. At first, they even tried to use strong-arm tactics. The three of them would grab a drunk and bundle him off. Sometimes, they would have to use their fists. But it never worked. And it was not long before they realized that they could not force other people to get sober. Instead, they decided to lead sober lives themselves and be available to any alcoholic who needed and wanted help. That paid off, and A.A. began to grow slowly but steadily in the city.

At first, they had held small meetings in their homes. But as their numbers grew they began to rent the cheapest space they could find. They would comb the Salvation Army for old chairs and a used refrigerator, and sometimes even a coffee urn. Their meeting rooms were gritty and without pretense. As the fellowship grew, so did the number of meetings. And now there were meetings in the city three nights a week. On other nights, most members traveled to meetings in other towns.

Jim was immediately swept up in the life of A.A. He and Fred went to a meeting every night, but they never went to the meetings together. Fred had learned how to drive after he left Guest House, and a car was assigned to him. He would generally pick up two or three people to take to the meeting with him. Jim could not drive so he took his favorite form of transportation, the taxicab. The two men were very close, but they decided to travel to meetings separately in order to keep from insulating themselves from the rest of the fellowship. They were great pals as Jim said, but they did not want to let their friendship interfere with meeting other alcoholics. At the end of each day, however, they would meet in one of their rooms and discuss their progress.

"I feel like I'm just taking," Fred said one night.

"So do I, but I'm enjoying it," Jim replied.

"I want to do more," Fred said.

"How much more can you do? They're probably going to let you go back to teaching next semester. Bill Donahue already hinted that I might be able to teach 'Evidences of Christianity.' If we start teaching again, there are going to be papers and meetings and counseling sessions. There's not going to be an awful lot of time to do more in A.A."

Fred pondered Jim's words.

"I've thought of that," he said. "But I'm beginning to think there's more to A.A. then what we've been doing, and there's more to get than we've been getting. They talk about the joy of living, and that's something that escapes me. People look at me and they say 'There goes Fred. He's like Sad Sack in the comics.' "

Jim smiled because it was true. Fred did seem to walk under a somber cloud.

"But I think that if I really get involved in A.A., something's going to happen to me. I think there's a chance that I could get rid of this emptiness."

"Why not just help the students? Turn the young barbarians into Christians?" Jim said.

"Almost any Jesuit on this hill can do that," Fred answered. "I think God is calling me to something else. And I think he may be calling you, too."

Jim laughed. "I have a feeling that I don't want to answer the telephone and find out what he wants."

"Well this is what I think — and I may be wrong. I probably am wrong. But this is what I think. There are many, many people out there who are lost. They're drunks and they don't know they're drunks. They're in prison because of crimes that they committed because of alcohol. Or they're in insane asylums being treated for psychosis when in fact their disease is alcoholism."

"So?"

"We're fishers of men."

"Yeah, Fred, but A.A. isn't allied with any particular religion. If you make it Catholic or even Christian you're going to screw things up."

"I think we can keep the two things separate. It's a spiritual program. We're spiritual people. As members of A.A., we're not trying to convert people to Catholicism. We're trying to help them recover from a disease which has a spiritual component. They need a power greater than themselves. I'm not going to tell them who that power is. I'm just going to tell them the power is there and wants to help them.

"But," Fred continued, "if along the way, I meet a Catholic who needs a priest, I'll be there to help him, too."

Jim was silent only for a moment.

"What are you suggesting?" he asked.

"That one of us starts visiting prisons and the other starts visiting asylums."

"Just like that."

"Yes."

"Out of the blue."

"Yes."

"Stone cold sober."

"Yes."

"I knew I shouldn't have picked up the phone," Jim said.

Fred appeared disheartened.

"You're not interested?"

"Oh, what the hell," Jim said. "Jesuits are supposed to have heroic virtue. What do you want, the prisons or the nut houses?"

"Jails scare me," Fred said. "So I'll take them and you can have the asylums."

Chapter Three

The locked wards were very frightening at first. They were in fact like bedlam. There was a darkness there that no amount of electricity could dispel. Sometimes the insane seemed almost to be acting, as if they were willful children playing at a game which Jim could not fathom. And sometimes they seemed to be propelled by an inner malignancy which defied reason and humanity. Jim entered the locked wards the way someone who fears water wades into the surf, hesitantly, fearfully, ready to turn and run, except that the door had been locked behind him, and there was no where to go except into the deeper water.

"Are you Jesus?" a woman asked him. She wore a white bathrobe and slippers, and her hair had not been combed.

They stood in a long day room with a few card tables and chairs scattered about. Against one wall there was a tattered sofa which had large dark urine stains. Even though they were on the fourth floor, the windows were barred. Jim looked behind him. The door was locked, and he was in a room with about two dozen maniacs. He was not alone. There were three white-clad attendants — two men and a woman — present, but they ignored his presence. Indeed, Jim could feel their hostility.

"Does he look like Jesus, you stupid bitch?" a man shouted at her.

The woman ignored the comment.

"I'm looking for Jesus. Are you Jesus?" She seemed worried, almost distraught.

"Perhaps I can help you find him," Jim said. "Why are you looking for him?"

"I'm his mother. I sent him out for a newspaper, and he hasn't come back. That was hours ago. But they won't let me go out to look for him. Did you see him out there?"

"Not today," Jim said.

"If you see him, tell him I want him," the woman said.

A large man approached Jim and stared at him.

"I want a fuggin' cigarette," he said. His arms were folded across his chest. He needed a shave, and he stared at Jim in a challenging, mocking way.

"You can't smoke in here," Jim answered.

"I killed my father," the man said.

"Oh?"

"With a hammer."

"Oh."

"Are you a father?"

"I'm a priest, yes."

"I don't like fathers."

"I gathered that," Jim said.

"You're lucky I don't have a hammer."

"Yes."

"Or I'd beat your brains out all over the floor."

"That's enough out of you," Jim said. "Get out of my way."

The man looked surprised, but he moved.

"That's the only way you can treat that guy, Father."

Jim turned to look at the man who spoke. He was shorter than Jim and a few years younger. He had a hang-dog look as if he had been sad for a very long time.

"What are you doing in here?" Jim asked.

The man shrugged.

"I'm crazy," he said.

"You are?" Jim was puzzled. "How so? I mean just what's wrong?"

"How do I know? They say I have chronic depression."

"What are they doing for you?"

"They give me shock treatments. I've had twenty-eight of them," the man said.

"But why do they have you locked up?"

"It's part of the routine."

"Routine?" Jim asked.

"Yeah," the man explained. "There's a regular routine. The police pick me up. The judge sends me to the state hospital for an indeterminate period. They give me shock treatments and stick me in with the really sick ones. After a month or so they move me out into the regular population, and after a while they let me out. And then, sooner or later the police pick me up again."

"What do the police pick you up for?"

"Being drunk. I guess I get drunk because I'm chronically depressed."

"Or because you're like me," Jim said.

"Like you?" the man seemed mystified as if they could not possibly have any common ground.

"Yes. Like me. I'm an alcoholic."

"An alcoholic, Father? A drunk? Is that why you're in here?"

"Yes," Jim said, "but I'm just visiting. Have you ever been to A.A.?"

"You mean the automobile thing where you get the free road service?"

Jim laughed and it was the man's turn to be puzzled.

"No. That's triple A. This is Alcoholics Anonymous. It's a place for people like you and me. We go there to stop drinking and we get better."

"I'm not drinking," the man said. "But I'm not getting any better."

"Well, if you come to A.A. maybe you will."

"I can't get better. I'll never get better. It isn't just booze. I've got this buzzing in my head," the man said. "And it feels like I got a steel band wrapped around my skull digging into my temples."

"How long have you had that?"

"I don't know. Years I guess. The only time it goes away is when I drink or after I have a shock treatment. Sometimes it's so bad, I can't even think-or hear or even talk. That's when they grab me. They scramble my brains. And then you get these convulsions. They're sort of like the dry heaves only ten times worse."

"How long have you been coming to this place?"

"I don't know. I told this judge where he could go one morning. And the next thing I know I'm here and they got me on a table and they stick this thing in my mouth so I won't bite my tongue and zap. Boy, I'll tell you I never said anything to a judge again. But they still send me here. Once you get on the list it's like being a yo-yo. You keep getting snapped back in this place. There's guys I know that are on the jail list. Whenever they get picked up, the judge sends them to the county jail. The guys on the jail

list wish they were on the nut house list, and the nut
house guys wish they were on the jail list."

"Jesus," the woman screamed.

"Shut up you bitch. I'll beat your brains out your fuggin' ears and all over your shoulders, and then I'll stuff
them in your mouth. And you'll never scream again," the
man who wanted the cigarette roared.

"Jesus," the woman screamed.

"Where's the nurse? Put her in isolation. Nurse?
Nurse?" another woman shouted from a corner.

"It's like this all the time. That's why I wish I was on
the jail list," the man said.

"What's your name?" Jim asked.

"Anthony."

"Italian?"

"Lithuanian."

"I'm Father Jim, Anthony. And I'm going to try to
come here almost every day."

"Are you nuts, too? Did they just stick you in here?
You're not a priest are you. I've been talking to another
nut."

"I'm a priest, Anthony. A Jesuit. And unlike you and
the rest of these people, I can come and go as I wish."

"Why would anybody wish to come here? We're all
wishing to get out."

Jim looked around the ward. He had no answer for
Anthony. It was a hopeless place, much more hopeless
than any place he had ever been before. There was no
conceivable reason why anyone with the slightest vestige
of sanity would want to come to a place like this.

"I don't know," he said finally. "Maybe just to say
'hello.' "

"You ready, Father?"

A male attendant wandered over and unlocked the

door. Jim felt as if he was being forced to leave, but he did not protest.

"Yes," he answered.

The attendant waited for Jim to step through the door and then he locked it behind them.

"This is the end of the line, Father. Most of them never come back once they get this far. There's nothing anybody can do for them. We feed them, and we wipe their shit off them — pardon my French, Father — but that's what we do — and we keep them from killing each other."

Jim nodded.

"Every once in a while, we get somebody like you who decides maybe they can help. So they come, maybe once, maybe twice, and then they give up, and we never see them again. God gave up on these people. You know that? They ain't even people, really, Father. They ain't. They're animals."

"How come you have the men and the women together?"

"That's only for a few hours during the day. It calms them down. Believe it or not. Of course they're calmer when the Blessed Virgin is in isolation."

Jim stared at the man.

"I'm sorry, Father. You get a little — what do they call it — jaded in this place. They call her that because she says she's Jesus' mother. It really don't mean anything. No offense."

They came to the elevator, and the attendant pushed the down button.

"It'll be here in a second, Father. I gotto get in there in case all hell breaks loose," he said. "Good-bye, Father."

"See you tomorrow," Father Jim replied.

The attendant just shook his head.

— ✧ —

The lobby was filled with people, some of them visitors, some of them patients. Near the front door, a man was genuflecting and blessing himself, but no one paid him any attention. The lobby was ringed with chairs with wooden arms and imitation leather cushions. Most of them were occupied by patients, men and women, who sat staring sullenly at nothing. The gloom, was offset in Jim by a sudden feeling of elation — a recognition that he could leave this place of torment — and he began to smile.

"There is nothing funny here, Father."

He turned and faced a young woman, probably in her early twenties, whose face reflected a profound melancholy.

"I wasn't laughing. I was rejoicing. I could just as easily be an inmate. There are probably people here who aren't as sick as I was who will never get out," he said.

"Were you crazy, Father?"

"Not like most of the people here. But I was pretty sick. I'm an alcoholic. A drunk."

The young woman wore no makeup and her hair had not been combed. She wore a brown sweater that was worn at the elbows and a cheap gray skirt.

"What's your name?" Jim asked.

"Kathleen."

"What are you doing here?"

She pulled up the sleeves of her sweater and showed him her scarred wrists.

"I see," Jim said. "What was the matter?"

"Sometimes things just get black, Father. I have this huge pit inside of me, and I crawl into it. And it gets deeper and darker and deeper and darker. And I can't get out. The only way I can escape it is by dying."

She was so forlorn, so wounded. He felt a tremendous warmth toward her, and he took one of her hands in his and began to pat it.

"There's no one, Father. No friends. Nobody. My family doesn't want to see me. I'm alone. Just alone."

He continued to pat her hand, and he looked at her as if he was entranced. She hardly noticed.

"I need a friend, Kathleen," he said.

"Oh, bullshit, Father."

Jim looked hurt and dropped her hand.

"Really? Or are you feeling sorry for me?" she asked.

"Really."

"And you want me to be your friend?" Her tone was incredulous and carried a hard edge.

"Why not?"

"Nobody wants me. You gotta be kidding."

"Nobody wants me either," Jim said.

"Really?"

"Really."

The two of them went to the cafeteria and had coffee and talked for almost forty-five minutes. As Jim was preparing to leave, Kathleen touched his arm.

"Something I haven't told you, Father."

"Yes?"

"One of the doctors here thinks I'm an alcoholic, too."

"O, my prophetic soul," Jim said with a huge smile.

"Your what?"

"I knew it," Jim said. "I had a feeling."

"Yeah, but what did you just say."

"It's a line from a play. Hamlet."

"Aren't we a little, sort of, different to be friends?"

"Why?"

"You're a Jesuit, and I'm in a state hospital."

"So what?"

"So why would you want to be my friend?"

Jim thought for a minute.

"There is a beauty in you that I find very attractive."

"Me?" she asked in disbelief.

Jim nodded solemnly, and then he walked down the steps to the waiting taxicab.

Chapter Four

Kathleen was a brat. She sat at the cafeteria table clicking the salt and pepper shakers together and singing an off-key version of "Three Blind Mice." Occasionally she would interrupt the song for a brief monologue.

"This place stinks. The food stinks. The doctors stink. The people stink. The johns stink. The attendants stink. The patients stink. Everything stinks."

Then she would resume singing "Three Blind Mice," keeping rhythm by clicking the shakers.

Anthony was a groaner.

He sat directly across the table from Kathleen with his head in his hands. Whenever she would stop her song, he would emit a soft but tortured groan.

Jim was at a loss. He was embarrassed and frustrated. His presence at the state hospital seemed futile, almost self-defeating. The more he visited the place, the less sure he became of himself and of his mission.

"Oooooh," Anthony groaned.

"Father, why don't you get us passes and we'll all go down to the bar on the corner and have a few drinks?" Kathleen asked.

Jim looked at her to see if she was joking.

"Why not, Father. Lots of the people around here do that. If you go to the bar across from the main gate, you can't tell who are the attendants and who are the patients."

"Oooooh," Anthony said.

"Boy, would I like a nice tall beer with a shot next to it. A couple of them," Kathleen said. "Come on, Father. What are we doing sitting here? Can't you see? This is a day that was made for drinking."

The windows in the cafeteria were small and set ten feet above the floor. Jim looked up, but he could not tell if it was sunny or whether it was still cloudy out.

"See? God made this day to drink. On the seventh day he rested and on the eighth day he drank. Or maybe he drank on the seventh day, and he rested on the eighth day, but the Bible doesn't mention it because they don't want us to know about that," Kathleen said.

"You know what would happen if I got you a pass and you went out and drank?"

"Come on, Father. Don't give me that bullshit. Who cares what happens? What can they do to me? Stick a mouthpiece between my teeth and jolt the hell out of me? So what? It's worth it just to get away from these jerks. They are jerks, Father. You have to admit that."

"They're trying, Kathleen."

"You think so. Really? They get all these foreign doctors who can't even speak English. All they do is sit around and eat and drink coffee and then they get their jollies by frying peoples' brains. I mean they're a bunch of goddam sadists. Sorry, Father, I didn't mean to swear. But that's what they are, and you know it."

"Oooh," Anthony said.

"I mean, look at poor Anthony. What do they do for this poor slob? Does that buzzing in his head come from him being crazy, or does it come from the twenty-eight shock treatments he's had. Twenty-eight shock treatments. Can you imagine what their electric bills are? If they'd give us the money they spend on electricity, instead of jolting the living daylights out of everybody, we could have one hell of a party, Father."

"Oooooh," Anthony said. His face was contorted with pain, and he closed his eyes and pressed his fingertips into his skull.

"Can you imagine? A portable bar. Ten of them. You could wheel in a table full of champagne buckets. That would do more for everyone here than all the electric shock treatments in the world."

Jim was not paying attention. He was staring, with a feeling of helplessness, at Anthony.

"Have you ever been to one of the parties here? They hang up some crepe paper and bring out a phonograph. And the only people who dance are the real psychos and they only dance by themselves. Sometimes the attendants will try to dance with you, but they only try to rub up against you. You know what I mean?

"They've only got one thing on their minds and you better not get caught in a dark hallway. They do more deflowering around here than people who take down wall-paper for a living."

Jim reached across the table and circled Anthony's head with his hands. He closed his eyes and prayed silently.

"And the doctors and the nurses are always grabbing each other in the corridors. There is more sex in this place than your average Paris bordello."

No one noticed, neither Kathleen nor any of the people at the other tables, but Jim would not have cared if they had. His heart went out to Anthony in his pain. The doctors and the treatment could not help Anthony. Jim could do nothing for him. He was beyond human help. He was in too much pain even to hear the message of A.A. Jim felt as desperate as the groaning man. If he could not help Anthony, what was the sense of coming to the hospital? Miracles were not within the realm of Jim's experience, but Anthony needed a miracle. So Jim prayed, quietly and insistently.

"I've had some narrow escapes from these people. A couple of times Fat Louey tried to grab me. The guy is so repulsive. I mean he smells," Kathleen said.

When Jim finished praying, Anthony looked at him in disbelief.

"What did you do?"

Jim was afraid that he had made things worse, and he didn't answer.

"Where did it go?"

"Where did what go?" Kathleen asked.

"The buzzing," Anthony said. "I don't hear it anymore. And that feeling like I had a steel band digging into my temples, that's gone too."

"Now there's a reason to celebrate," Kathleen said.

Jim smiled at Anthony.

"What d'ya say Father Jim. Why don't you get us passes and we'll go out and celebrate?" Kathleen implored.

"Not today, Kathleen."

"Tomorrow?"

"Don't worry about tomorrow. Let tomorrow take care of itself."

"Thank you, Father. I can't believe it but thank you. These doctors are really going to think I'm nuts," Anthony said.

"Don't tell them. Just say that it went away," Jim said.

"Don't tell them? That's right. Why should I tell them? What do they care? This is unbelievable, Father. This is like a miracle."

"You know, you don't have to get carried away, Anthony," Kathleen said. "It will probably come back tomorrow."

Anthony looked frightened.

"Don't worry about tomorrow. You're all taken care of."

"Are you sure?"

"I'm sure."

As Jim was leaving the hospital, he had a sudden intense feeling of joy.

"Who was in greater need of that," he wondered as he climbed into the cab, "Anthony or me?"

And then there was a moment of disappointment.

"She never really noticed," Jim thought. "She didn't understand."

Just before midnight, Fred came to Jim's room.

"Still up?" he asked.

"Yeah. I only got back about twenty minutes ago."

"Me too," Fred said. "How did it go today?"

"Awful."

"That bad?"

"It's the land of the lost. They should put up that sign that says 'Abandon all hope you who enter here.' "

"Medieval?"

"I keep expecting to stumble into a snake pit," Jim said. "They really are insane. It's not like alcoholism. They're really nuts. Most of them. Not all. There's a guy, a man named Anthony. He's alcoholic and they're treating him like he's psychotic. And a girl — Kathleen. But they'd probably be better off if they were really crazy because they're not getting any help. They just keep them there for a while, scramble their brains with shock treatments and send them back to their local gin mill."

"Sounds promising," Fred said.

Jim laughed. "Things any better among the felons?"

"I'm up to my ears in red tape. They must think that a priest recovering from alcoholism is a real danger to them."

"Another do-gooder," Jim said. "That's what they think I am. And they're sure that I'm going to give up in a week or so."

"Are you?"

"Not until I am absolutely sure that I'm wasting my time."

"That reminds me of a conversation I had with Sister Liz Mary. I used to wonder whether it did any good to come and see you at the hospital," Fred said. "You seemed to be unreachable. And you never showed the least bit of progress or even gave any sign that you knew that I was there. But something inside of me told me it was important to keep coming. So I did even though it didn't seem to do any good."

"Persistence. Maybe that's the key," Jim said. "I've been thinking of buying some coffee and doughnuts and putting on a meeting."

"Oh really?"

"Yeah. And you're going to be my first speaker."

"God help them," Fred said.

— ✧ —

As usual, Jim had trouble getting to sleep. His back ached and he had had too much coffee. At some moments he could almost hear the footsteps of Sister Liz Mary in the hall and the click of her rosary beads. The loneliness had seemed so absolute, the pain so inexorable. There had been no escape, and yet he had escaped.

But now he was in another alien place. He was not teaching. His participation in the life of the Jesuit community was minimal. Instead of being one of those dynamic Jesuits he had always longed to be, he was spending most of his time at meetings of Alcoholics Anonymous and visiting the locked wards of hospitals. Perhaps his vocation was a waste. Perhaps he was such a failure that God would count him a success if only he did not die in the gutter.

As his mind began to drift, he noticed an image at the periphery of his consciousness. He knew what it was. It had been there the night before and the night before that. It was the image of Kathleen — silent, ambiguous. He did not summon it. He did not entertain it. It was just there.

Chapter Five

His name was Daniel but they called him Silent Cal. He had been bouncing in and out of jails and state hospitals for twenty years. He had been divorced, disowned and disinherited. The police had made it clear to him that he was unwelcome in his home town, and they told him that his family wanted it that way. He never saw his children, and his only friends were the winos he met and drank with in doorways and railroad cars and fields with long grass — the weeds. That was where he came from and where he went — the weeds. And when he was not in jail or in a state hospital, he nickled and dimed until he had the price, and then he stopped asking strangers for money and bought a bottle of muscatel. If he could not get wine, he would buy mouthwash. If he could get nothing else, he would find sterno. His days were spent in either anxiety or alcoholic haze; his nights were spent either in oblivion or jails cells. When he was thrown in jail and his body was deprived of alcohol, he would suffer delirium tremens and sometimes grand mal seizures. Usually, the cops did not care. They would let him writhe on the floor and foam at the mouth, and then in the morning they would check to see if he was still alive. On the rare occasions when he spoke, he referred to the police and to jail guards as screws.

He had come to the meeting because he had been told there would be fresh doughnuts, hot coffee, and free cigarettes. He had been to meetings before. Sometimes he wandered into them on cold nights just to be warm. Sometimes he had been dragged to them by members of his family. He never paid much attention. And he was not paying much attention now. He took three doughnuts in his left hand and a cup of coffee in his right and slipped quietly to a corner. He stood closed in upon himself, his shoulders hunched and half-turned to the wall, insulating himself from the eight other people in the room.

Jim was standing with Anthony and Kathleen, but he was watching Silent Cal. He was one of those rare patients that even the doctors agreed was simply alcoholic. He was, they said, a hopeless case, a man who would either die in the gutter or suffer a wet brain. Jim had seen wet brains. Sections of their minds were irretrievably gone, their memories, their true emotions. They lived in a mist, a kind of never-never land where they had lost everything, even the recollection of themselves. Silent Cal had been in almost every institution in the state with the exception of the state prison. He had on three occasions done six month terms at Bridgewater State Hospital — or Bridgie as the drunks called it — a warehouse for the criminally insane. The hospital also housed incorrigible drunkards and wet brains. Silent Cal had liked Bridgewater. He worked in the

library and made friends with a few of the other drunks.
One of them was a priest, another a doctor and another a
lawyer. At Bridgewater he had been in good company.

"I'm Father Jim."

Silent Cal's hands and mouth were full. He could neither take the hand which Jim offered him nor speak.

"That's all right. That's all right," Jim said. "I just
wanted to introduce myself and thank you for coming."

Silent Cal gave him the standard blank institutional
look.

"You're helping me a lot," Jim said.

Silent Cal's face remained blank.

"It's really good to see you. Maybe a little later I can
introduce you to my friends, Anthony and Kathleen."

Silent Cal cleared his throat but said nothing.

Kathleen walked up to them, but she completely
ignored Silent Cal.

"Father Fred wants to know if you're ready?"

"This is my friend Kathleen," Jim said.

There was no response, not even a nod.

"Come on, Father," Kathleen said. "Let's get the show
on the road. What d'ya say?"

"See you later," Jim said.

This time the blank institutional look was replaced
with a slight grimace.

Only Jim and Anthony paid attention while Fred
spoke. Silent Cal had three more doughnuts and then
dozed off in a chair in a corner. Kathleen crossed and
recrossed her legs and frequently emitted audible sighs.
Two elderly ladies carried on a whispered conversation.
There were two other men in the room. One was about
fifty years old. He stared straight ahead as if in a trance.
The other could have been any age between forty and seventy. He was about five-feet four-inches tall but his

clothes were intended for a much bigger man. His sleeves extended past his finger tips and his trouser legs dragged on the floor. He paced up and down near the dozing Silent Cal. He walked quickly, making tight turns while talking quietly to himself.

At one point the man brushed against Silent Cal.

"Get away from me you crazy bastard," Silent Cal said. He kept his eyes open long enough to make sure that the man moved to the other side of the room, and then he dozed off again.

"It's been a good meeting. Thank you all for coming," Jim said when Fred finished speaking. "We're going to meet here again next week at the same time. Now for those of you who care to join me, let's close the meeting with The Lord's Prayer."

At first, only Anthony and Father Fred cared to join him. Toward the middle of the prayer, however, Kathleen added her voice to the others. Silent Cal had already disappeared by the time they finished.

"Pretty grim," Fred said.

"A good reminder," Jim responded.

"You're really gonna do this again next week?" Kathleen asked.

"Yes," Jim said.

"You know, Father, sometimes I have to ask myself who's crazy and who's not around this place."

Jim laughed.

"Even if nobody else got anything. Even if everybody slept or paced or talked and nobody paid attention, I got something," Jim said.

"Yeah," she said, "a feeling of futility."

"Father, you mean to say that I don't have any power at all when it comes to booze — that willpower does no good?"

Anthony had emerged from deep thought and was looking at Fred.

"If you're an alcoholic, you are powerless over alcohol," Fred said. "And you can't stay away from it by yourself."

"Is that right?" Anthony asked Jim.

Jim nodded.

"That explains all those times that I got drunk when I didn't want to," Anthony said.

Jim nodded again.

"But tell me, Father, am I nuts or not?"

"Well, we're all nuts. You, me, Fred. But not like the people in here are nuts. We're only crazy when it comes to alcohol. If we stop drinking and follow a few simple suggestions, we can be as sane as anyone in the world, and we never have to come back to a place like this unless we want to so we can help others."

"Are you serious?" Kathleen said in sarcastic disbelief.

Jim nodded very earnestly.

"You think the only reason I'm in here is because I don't have any power when it comes to booze?"

"That's right," Jim said.

She shook her head. "Oh, I don't know, Father. I don't think I care for what you're telling me. You're dangerous. You want me to stop drinking — forever. That's crazy."

"Would you rather spend the rest of your life bouncing in and out of these places? Would you rather end up like Silent Cal?"

"Come on, Father. Me? Like Silent Cal?"

"It's a progressive disease, Kathleen. We get sicker."

"That's fine for you to say. You're old. I'm just a kid. I'm only twenty-three."

"They didn't start putting me into hospitals until I was forty-five," Jim said. "You're way ahead of me."

Kathleen was wide-eyed and disbelieving.

Fred, who had been quiet, suddenly spoke.

"Wouldn't you prefer to be an alcoholic and be able to do something about yourself rather than one of these poor people who are never going to get any better?" he asked.

"And not drink?" she asked. "And not drink?"

"And not drink," Fred said.

"I don't know," Kathleen answered. "Yes, I do. Neither. I don't want to be an alcoholic or crazy. I don't want to be either one."

Now it was Anthony who interjected himself. "You already are. You can't change it. It's too late."

"Oh, Anthony. Shut up. Will you? Have you joined them? I mean what's the matter with you? Are you a member of A.A. now?"

"If they'll take me," Anthony said.

"Oh my God. Oh my God. Last week you were walking around with a buzzing in your head, and now you're a member of A.A. What in the world is going on?"

Without admitting it to himself, Jim preferred the medical hospital to the state hospital. He felt more like a priest where there were nuns in the corridors and crucifixes on the walls. Just as he made his rounds among the psychiatric patients, each day he would come to St. Vincent's and visit the sick and the suffering. Jim was a specialist. The hospital had its own Catholic chaplain, a priest assigned from the diocese, so Jim concentrated only on patients who were hospitalized because of alcohol. Many of them were on the psychiatric floor. Some were merely run down, some were jaundiced, and some were dying from liver disease or ailments caused by their alcoholism.

"I'm Father Jim, and I'm an alcoholic," he would say to a startled patient.

The response was frequently one of disbelief. Sometimes his declaration was received with a shrug as if to say 'you too?' and sometimes with a shake of the head as if a negative moral judgment was being pronounced.

It was in the medical units that Jim could see the true nature of the disease. Behind the smiles and the tears, behind the toasts and good fellowship, behind the broken families and the ruined careers, there was death-thin bodies with yellow faces, cracked lips, shaking hands, the looks that said, 'Life is over, there is only the final agony to contend with and I'll be gone.' Sometimes Jim could feel the acceptance fill the room of the ruined warrior. It was almost tangible. It said, 'The battle is over — thank God. I have lost it, but who cares? There is peace in death.' Sometimes the face that looked up at him was very young. Sometimes it was ancient. There was often a kind of irrevocable beauty, a wisdom which comes only at the end — a wisdom which says, 'I have been to the mountain. I have seen the other side. It is better than here.'

Sometimes the end came suddenly.

"Father, I'm going," the voice was weak but clear and insistent.

"It's all right. God loves you. He's waiting for you," Jim said.

"Father, I need to go to confession."

"I absolve you of all your sins in the name of the Father, the Son, and the Holy Spirit."

"But Father, I haven't told you my sins."

"It's all right. They're forgiven. It's all taken care of. The debt's paid."

"Are you sure?" the man asked. He was at the edge of the abyss, and he knew it.

"Yes," Jim answered.

"You'd better be right," the man said. A moment later he was dead.

Sometimes he felt that he was doing the wrong thing. He was being drawn further and further from the classroom. During the day he was almost always away from the campus, visiting the hospitals, and at night, every night, he went to an A.A. meeting. He found that at times when he was alone, when he was dozing or just relaxing, the image of Kathleen would appear to him. Sometimes he would have imaginary conversations with her. Sometimes, he would just sit with her. He longed to comfort her, to heal her, to free her, to see her smile, to see her laugh.

He wondered what the other Jesuits would think if they knew that a young woman was occupying his quiet time with him. He wondered what they would think if they knew, what he hardly admitted to himself, that he loved her. He loved to be in her company and to talk with her. He enjoyed even her imaginary visits. Would the other priests think that he was an old lecher, that he wanted to violate his vow of celibacy, or would they understand? In his heart Jim knew that he loved Kathleen, but not in a way that was against his priesthood. He cherished her, almost as if she were his daughter. He cherished her friendship. He cherished her very life. It was a mystery to him how in the second half of his life he could find such beauty in a sick, self-centered and seemingly very plain and awkward young woman. But he did. Beneath everything, she had a beauty and a grace which attracted him. She was a gift in his life.

And then there were all the people he visited, the sick and the dying, the drunks and the crazy people. What did that have to do with being a Jesuit or even, really, of being a sober alcoholic. Other men got sober and returned to their careers. Lawyers practiced law, doctors practiced medicine, and teachers taught. Not Jim. He spent his days with the flotsam and jetsam, people who sometimes could not connect two thoughts, people who were blind to their own disease, people who had discarded most of their humanity. First Class Collins was spending his days with the outcasts, with the socially unacceptable. It seemed so out of character.

One night as he was falling asleep, some words edged to his consciousness: "Visit the sick. Comfort the afflicted. Heal the brokenhearted."

He had had too much coffee, again. His back ached, but he was not restless.

The room was still. His mind began to drift off.

He heard a voice. He thought it was out in the hall.

"Follow me," the voice said.

"Who's out there?" Jim asked. "They ought to be in bed."

A feeling of deep peace came over him, and a moment later he was asleep.

Chapter Six

It took only a few months for Jim to assemble a coterie. He did not make a conscious effort to choose its members; they were attracted to him, as he was to them. At first there were only Anthony and Kathleen. Jim had gone to the administrator of the hospital and received permission to take the two out to meetings. He would arrive at dusk by taxicab, and they would be waiting in the lobby. Often, he would first take them to a restaurant for dinner before going to the meeting. Anthony had been eager to go along with Jim, but it had not been easy to get Kathleen to join them. She had at first been adamant in her refusal.

"People in A.A. are not going to bite you," Jim told her.

"I know that. There's you and Father Fred. I know they're probably all like you," she said, adding after a pause, "Loveable and a bit off."

Jim ignored the comment.

"Then why won't you come along?"

"Sometimes you're dumb, Father," she said.

"Ah," he said, suddenly enlightened. "Come on, we'll stop at a department store."

"Really?"

"Certainly."

They bought several sweaters, skirts and blouses. Jim charged them to the college.

"Are you going to get in trouble, Father?" Kathleen asked as they walked out to the street. She was wearing a new outfit. Her old clothes were in a bag which she pushed into a trash barrel.

"Trouble?"

"You know, for charging this stuff to the college."

"Not at all," Jim said. "Not at all. They can afford it."

And, indeed, no one in the Jesuit community ever mentioned the purchases to Jim. Perhaps no one wanted to ask about them. Jim was beginning to be looked upon as just a bit eccentric. There were the monthly cab bills. And there was, after all, the coterie. Jim would bring his friends to the priests' dining hall for lunch or for coffee in the late afternoon. They would sit at a table in a corner and wolf down Danish pastries, drink many cups of coffee, and often fill the room with laughter.

In addition to Kathleen and Anthony, they were often joined by Bobby. Bobby was in real estate and horses and drove a new 1961 Cadillac. Before he met Jim, he drove a Corvette, but late one night after leaving a bar, he drove it into a tree at ninety miles an hour. Even the doctors did not know how Bobby survived. He had broken both legs, both arms, and most of his ribs, fractured his spine in three places, fractured his skull, and broken his nose and his jaw. It had taken three hours to get him out of the car, but Bobby did not notice because he had passed out. Sister Liz

Mary had told Jim about Bobby and Jim had visited his room. Bobby was in traction. His arms were in casts and his head was swathed in bandages.

"Hi. I'm Father Jim."

"Hi," came the response.

"How did you manage this?"

"What?"

"Hitting a tree at ninety miles an hour."

"You wouldn't understand, Father."

"Why not?"

"You'd have to be an alcoholic to understand."

"I am."

"You are?"

"Yes."

"In A.A.?"

"Yes."

"You still probably won't understand."

"Try me."

"I left a bar, and I decided to accelerate as much as I could and to keep the wheel perfectly straight."

"I understand."

"And I was going ninety when I came to a bend in the road."

"But you kept the wheel perfectly straight."

"Exactly."

"You wanted to commit suicide?"

"Not in those words. I just didn't want to keep living. Can you understand that?"

"Of course I can," Jim said. "Alcoholics are walking paradoxes. We want one thing but do something else. Or we do something that causes the exact opposite of the result we intend. It's all part of this insidious disease. It's almost heroic the kind of stuff we have to put up with inside of ourselves, never mind what's going on outside of us."

"Are you kidding?" Bobby asked.

"No. No," Jim protested. "This is a damnable disease. Imagine an illness which would take a nice prosperous young man with everything to live for and cause him to try to kill himself. It's insidious. It's vicious. It's damnable."

And Bobby would spend long hours reflecting on those words.

He was in the hospital for four months, and Jim visited him every day. He heard his confession, brought him Communion and listened to his complaints, his fears, and his hopes. And even as Bobby found a friend in Jim, Jim found a friend in Bobby, and he would tell the broken young man of his own interests, and especially of his two heroes, Babe Ruth and Thomas More — an unlikely pair, certainly, but they were the men who appealed to Jim. The Sultan of Swat had come to his hometown once when Jim was a kid, and he had gone to see him at the local theater. On stage, dressed in a suit, Ruth had seemed out of place, and yet there was something charismatic about him, some unspoken empathy between him and his audience, as if the Babe was pursuing their dream and they were pursuing his, as if baseball and home runs were a kind of mystical allegory for life, as if together they were seeking the Holy Grail. And the Bambino was burdened by alcohol and by the defects in his nature. Jim understood, and so did Bobby.

More was another story altogether. He was brilliant, a true Renaissance man, a politician and scholar, who was loyal to the Pope and the Church, with a great sense of humor and on top of all that he had two wives — in succession, of course. He was a man who stood up for what he believed in, even to the point of being beheaded, but a man, who even at the very end, had kept his wit and his sense of honor. Jim could spend hours telling stories about

St. Thomas, and Bobby, who was in great discomfort, was transported from his pain and surroundings to another time and to the presence of a heroic figure.

By the time Bobby got out of the hospital, Anthony and Kathleen had been released from the state hospital, and together with Father Jim, they made a very unlikely quartet. They were in one sense Quixotic and free-floating, and in another they were as serious as people who are under a sentence of death.

Anthony was unlettered, and often appeared to be in a daze, but he listened intensely to what people said as if he was afraid that he would miss some momentous truth. He was always ready to help set up a meeting or to clean up after one, and people noticed that newcomers to A.A. would often seek Anthony out and ask him questions. He seemed to have a gift for putting them at ease, and for giving them little insights into themselves and into alcoholism.

Kathleen was a pouter and a debater. Her most frequently used expression was 'you know.' She used it to begin her sentences, to punctuate them, to stress the most important points of her argument, and to fill in the silence when she paused. Sometimes when she spoke, people would try to count the number of times she used the two words, but usually they lost track, although one man insisted that she usually averaged one 'you know' every ten seconds. Her mind was like an unmade bed. It was rumpled and disorderly. It had lumps and smooth spots. Sometimes she would enunciate an idea with perfect clarity, and then suddenly wander off the track and become enmeshed in 'you knows' and 'I thinks' and 'I wonders' to the great distraction of her listeners. But she, too, had an intensity, and it was obvious from the outset that she was truly on the quest for sobriety.

Bobby was most unlike the other three. He liked money, good clothes, and expensive cars. He was a dreamer with hundreds of big plans and a gambler who loved the thrill of the track. He was gregarious, intelligent, sometimes insincere. Frequently, when he got up in the morning he would be sure that it was his last day in A.A., that at some point that day he would pick up a drink. He was filled with anger, remorse, and another pain which he could not identify, but he covered it all up by his ability to listen and to seem interested in the other person. He used Jim as a life preserver. Jim kept his head above the water. Jim gave him the impetus to go for one more day — to hang in there. It seemed he was forever hanging in there.

There was one thing that Bobby had in common with the other three. He was wounded. It was not that one leg was now shorter than the other and that he had to wear a special shoe and walk with a cane, or that he still experienced physical pain as a result of the crash. He suffered from an interior brokenness, a spiritual and emotional emptiness. It was easy to escape it during the day, riding around in a Cadillac with the other three or going to A.A. meetings. But late at night it was another story. It was then that the emptiness of his life attacked him, then that the absurdity of being Bobby with nothing to do except to drive a big car and go to meetings smothered him. It was then that life seemed meaningless and hopeless and then that the thought of death caressed him. Alone in the darkness with the shame of the past and the memory of defeat and foolishness, everything seemed futile. He would have to limp through life smiling and cracking jokes, nodding yes when he wanted to scream no. It was then that this God who was supposed to restore him to sanity seemed like an enemy. Why had the Maker of the Universe, the Creator of Bobby allowed all this to happen? If God loved him why did He let him get into the car that night? Why did He let him hit a tree? If God loved him, why was he an alcoholic? Why couldn't he just go out and have a few drinks and laugh like the rest of the world?

"Stop whining," Jim said at a meeting one night, after Bobby told him these thoughts. "You've got the 'poor me's.' That's your disease talking to you. It wants you to pick up a drink. It wants you to feel sorry for yourself and to resent God. It wants you to think you will never get better. And when you whine, you feed it."

"But Father," Bobby said, and indeed his voice did sound as if he was whining, "Look at me. I'm a cripple. I'm in pain. I'm an emotional basket case. I'm bankrupt spiritually. My girlfriend thinks I'm a bum; my old man says it was a mistake to sire me — he talks like I'm a frigging horse; my brothers ask me to keep a low profile, which means stay the hell away from them. I'm travelling with a couple of refugees from the state hospital — a girl who is absolutely bonkers — I mean she's nuts, Father — and an older guy who acts so dumb people think he's a retard. And with all due respect, a priest who's as crippled as I am and who can't even teach anymore."

"Oh anger. It will kill you. I'm glad you got it out. Thank God for that," Jim said.

"Thank God? Thank God?" Bobby said completely exasperated. "If it wasn't for God I wouldn't be in this mess. If God really cared about me, I wouldn't be an alcoholic. What do I have to thank him for? This? My life as a crippled drunk?"

"Thank him that the body is still warm," Jim said. "God didn't put the drink in your hand. God didn't drive your car into a tree. You did those things, not God, Bobby. And until you stop whining and start taking a good look at yourself, you're going to stay sick. And if you do, you'll pick up a drink. And maybe next time, you won't be so lucky or so blessed to come out of it with one leg shorter than the other. Maybe next time you'll come out of it with a leg amputated, or maybe you won't come out of it at all. If I were you, I'd stop blaming God for what I did, and I'd start thanking Him for what He did. He got you to A.A., and He's giving you a chance to turn your life around."

"Bobby's a pain in the ass, isn't he Father," Kathleen said.

She had waited until they finished talking and Bobby had walked away before she came over to Jim.

Jim laughed.

"He's like most of the people in my life. He makes me feel like I should go crawl under a rug," she said. "He despises me. Most people despise me. Everybody despises me. My father despises me. My family despises me. They don't want to have anything to do with me. Sometimes I think God despises me. You know that, Father?"

"I don't despise you," Jim said.

"Yeah. But you're different," Kathleen said. "It's your job. I mean, I'm just part of your quota."

"My what?"

"Your quota. You know. Yeah. Your quota."

"What quota?"

"You know. For lost sheep. That quota. Don't you have a quota? I mean, don't the Jesuits give you a quota?"

Jim wondered if there was a full moon. He looked out the window, but all he could see was the dark outline of a building across the alley.

"Kathleen, some Jesuits don't even speak to me. They think I'm a bum. They're afraid to let me teach. They lock the liquor cabinet when they see me coming. They think I'm a disgrace to the Society. They have no idea what I do at A.A. and they don't care."

"Then what are you doing here?"

Jim seemed puzzled.

"I mean, if they didn't send you, you know, what are you doing here?"

"I'm a drunk. If I want to stay sober, I have to come to A.A.," Jim said.

"But what about me? You know. How come you bought me those clothes? Why do you hang around with me? I mean, if I'm not part of a quota...."

"Kathleen," Jim said, "You're my friend. I love you."

"What?" She seemed surprised, almost shocked.

"I love you," Jim said. "I enjoy your company. I like being with you."

Kathleen's exterior shell had cracked. She seemed very vulnerable. "Me? Are you crazy? Nobody loves me."

"I do," Jim said.

She was on the verge of tears.

"Why?" she asked.

"Because you're loveable," Jim replied.

As Kathleen turned to walk away, she began to cry.

Anthony had been waiting, and he was on Jim almost immediately.

"They're having a tough time today," he said.

"Who?" Jim asked.

"Both of them."

"Yes," Jim admitted with a sigh.

"I'd be like that too, Father, if it wasn't for you."

"Me?"

"Yeah, Father. If you hadn't fixed my head," Anthony said. "If I still had that gole-darned buzzing, and if I still had that steel band pressing into my temples, I'd still be in the nuthouse. Sometimes I feel so lucky, Father, so blessed, that I want to scream 'Thank you' at the top of my lungs."

Jim smiled.

"You ought to tell them what a guy told me, Father. 'You can't be hateful, if you're grateful.' "

Jim laughed.

"I think maybe I'd better wait for the right moment," he said.

— ✧ —

As the meeting hall was emptying, Kathleen tugged on Father Jim's sleeve.

"Did you really mean what you said?" she asked.

"Of course," he said.

"Well I've been thinking, then. You know. I mean if you love me — I mean if some human being actually loves me — if you love me — and you're not kidding — and I'm not part of some Jesuit quota for finding lost sheep — if you really love me, just because, well, just because you love me — just because I'm me — then maybe, Father — I mean maybe — then it's possible — that God loves me?"

"Of course God loves you. You're the apple of his eye. He's nuts about you."

"Really, Father?" Kathleen asked with a big smile.

"Really," Jim said.

"I could float," Kathleen said. "I could just float right out of here."

— ✧ —

Bobby capped the night off.

"You were right," he said. "I have been whining. And I was right. She is bonkers. But that's all right. She's just a kid. And I'm bonkers, too," he said.

When they got to Bobby's car, Jim looked up at the sky. It was filled with the light of a brilliant full moon.

"Stop the car," Jim said.

"Right here?" Bobby asked. They were on the narrow road which went past the campus chapel.

"Yes," Jim said. "Pull over there and turn off the lights."

Bobby slipped the big car into a parking spot, and Jim rolled down his window. The sound of laughter and shouting voices reached them.

"Keep it down," a young man's voice whispered.

"Where are they?" Bobby asked.

"Up in the little cemetery?"

"What cemetery? You got a cemetery here?" he asked.

"Right over there," Jim said, pointing across the road to steps which were drenched in moonlight. They led up a small hill to an area which was surrounded by a stone wall.

"That's a cemetery?"

"That's where we plant the members of the Society," Jim said.

"Good grief," Kathleen said from the back seat. "Right in the middle of the campus?"

"Yes. Right up there. They'll stick me up there one of these days," he said.

"Right in the middle of everything?" Kathleen asked. "You'd think that if they had to bury people on campus they'd tuck them away in a corner, like over behind the football field."

"This probably was a corner when the college was started," Jim said. "But the campus kept growing and now this is at the center of things."

"What are we stopped for?" Anthony asked.

"Shhh," Jim said.

He took his cane and climbed out of the car, shutting the door gently behind him. The other three quickly followed. Jim walked slowly and carefully to the steps, with the others trailing him in Indian file.

"Whad'ya do with the church key?" a voice whispered.

"Quiet," another voice said. "You'll wake all the dead Jebbies."

There was muffled laughter.

"Whose turn is it?"

"Mine," a voice answered. "Let me finish this first."

"Chug it, will ya? If we stay out here too long we'll wake up the live Jebbies."

Jim and the others softly climbed the steps until they could see the small graveyard. It was only about forty yards long and twenty yards wide. Almost all of the white granite grave stones were alike. They were about two and a half feet high and rounded at the top. They were arrayed nine across in sixty rows.

"Are you the last?" another voice asked.

"No. He's next to last. I'm the last."

"Let's hurry it up. If they catch us we're gonna be in big trouble."

A clink resounded as one of the students set an empty beer bottle on top of a grave stone, and then suddenly a young man began to run through the cemetery, hurdling grave stone after grave stone. When he finished the sixty rows, another young man began to run and jump his way the length of the cemetery. At the last row, his toe caught the top of a grave stone and he crashed to the grass.

"Balls," he shouted.

There were gales of laughter from the other nine young men at the other end of the cemetery.

"Shut up, will ya?" a voice whispered harshly and urgently.

The student who fell picked himself up and trotted back to his friends.

"Is that it?" a voice asked.

"That's it."

"Are we out of beer?"

"Yeah."

"Then the full moon convocation of The Dead Jebby Hurdlers is now adjourned."

"Deo gratias," a voice responded.

The ten young men walked over to the stairs where Father Jim and the others stood. It was not until they were descending to the road that they realized they had witnesses. Not a word was said by either group as the students averted their faces and hurried down the steps. When they got to the road, the young men began to run.

"Holy shit," a voice rang out. "Was that a live Jebby or a dead Jebby?"

The other nine roared with laughter and kept running.

Chapter Seven

At first many of the old-timers thought that Father Jim was an eccentric. He seemed to collect the wounded the way a bag lady collects discarded scraps as she wanders from alley to alley and street to street. There was something bizarre about his retinue. Indeed, some of the people he collected were bag ladies and others were certifiably crazy. He would bring them to meetings and treat them with a deference which, outside of A.A., would have been reserved for the rich or the famous. It was not at all unusual to see the priest bringing coffee to a shabbily dressed woman reeking of body odor who had an insane glint in her eye and a pint of muscatel in her pocket. Jim would minister to the derelict with such solicitousness that sometimes the object of his attentions would begin to put on airs, even to become demanding as if Jim were merely a personal servant.

And he would laugh. That more than anything else was what initially upset the old-timers — his laugh — that and the fact that he seemed to be genuinely interested in these people, that he really seemed to like them, even to love them.

And, of course, there was the matter of Father Jim's attire. The longer he stayed around A.A., the shabbier he got.

"When is that suit going to be ready?" Bobby asked one noontime when Jim looked particularly shabby.

"What suit?" Jim asked.

"The suit I gave you the two hundred dollars for."

"Was that for a suit?" Jim asked.

The priest looked innocent, even naive, but Bobby suspected that it was a pretense.

"Of course it was for a suit. Don't you remember?"

"I just thought it was a gift," Jim said.

"God damn it, Father," Bobby said. He did not bother to ask the priest what happened to the money. He knew.

"Father, did you ever think that it might be a compulsion?"

"What?"

"Giving money away."

Jim laughed.

"You're the softest touch inside or outside A.A. Every bum in the city knows that. 'You need five bucks, go see Father Jim. It doesn't matter what you want to use it for, just go see him. Ask and you shall receive.' "

Jim laughed again.

Bobby was exasperated.

"Why do you do it?" he asked.

"It's something I learned from Kathleen," he said.

"Kathleen? She doesn't have a pot to piss in. Half the money you give away, you give to her," Bobby said.

"I learned how important it is to love people just the way they are, even bag ladies, Bobby. They think they are unlovable. They think that no one, not even God, cares about them or loves them. And, yes, sometimes I give them money."

"Sometimes?" Bobby said, his tone filled with incredulity.

"I only give it to people who need to know that they are loved," Jim said.

"Only those people? That's every friggin' person in the universe."

Jim laughed again.

"Look, Father. Let me be honest with you. Okay? People around here think you look like a bum. They say 'which one's the bag lady and which one's Father Jim?' "

This time Jim's laugh was louder and more prolonged. He seemed delighted.

"When we leave, Father, we're gonna go over to that ecclesiastical clothes place, and I'm gonna buy you a new suit and some new collars. And I'm gonna put the money in the guy's hand, and I'm gonna tell him the sale is final. No returns. No refunds."

Bobby walked away to get a cup of coffee. Father Jim did not notice him when he returned because his back was to Bobby as he talked to a man of about thirty.

"But Father," the man said, "I've got money."

"Of course you do," Father Jim agreed. "But it's all accounted for. It's for food. It's for the kids' clothes. You spend money on others, but you don't spend money on yourself. Here, take this," he said, handing the man a twenty dollar bill, "and spend it on yourself. Go out to dinner. Take your wife. Just spend it on having a nice time for yourself. Nothing else."

The man thought it over for a moment.

"Just me and my wife," he said.

"Yes. Enjoy yourselves."

"It's been a while," the man said, taking the twenty. "Thanks."

As they were leaving, Bobby touched Father Jim's arm.

"Can I ask you something, Father?

"Sure."

"How much money do you give away?"

The priest shook his head.

"I don't know," he said.

"You don't even have a rough idea?" Bobby asked.

"Love does not keep score," Jim answered.

Gradually, almost imperceptibly, the old timers began to accept Father Jim, not as just another recovering alcoholic, but as someone with a special gift for others in the fellowship. No one, however, was quite sure what that special gift was.

It was easy enough to accept Father Fred and to give him respect. Fred was an intellect. He was a man who studied things, chewed them over and over until he digested them, and if he did not understand, he asked. He was a man who could take a simple sentence in one of A.A.'s Twelve Steps of Recovery and explore it, plumb its depths, see things in it that others had not seen, and he was a man committed to the A.A. way. He never tried to impose his beliefs as a priest and a Catholic on the members of the fellowship; but at the same time his priesthood and his Catholicism remained the prominent features of his life. Fred was a quiet man; there was nothing flamboyant about him. About the only thing that called attention to himself was the way his head wagged whenever he felt stress. But despite his tendency to stay in the background, people were drawn to Fred. He was a man who listened and who understood, a man who could give effective counsel.

After a few years in the fellowship, Father Fred began to be approached frequently to do Fifth Steps. In that step, the recovering alcoholic admits to God, himself and another human being the exact nature of his wrongs. It is generally based on a written moral inventory which can take from a week to more than a year to complete. Fred was an exponent of leaving no rock unturned, of keeping nothing back, and generally when a person finished a Fifth Step with Fred, everything about the person down to the most shameful, most embarrassing incidents of the person's life had been discussed. The effect of that was that the past had been put in perspective, and the person had made a deep commitment to a new way of life.

When Fred spoke at meetings, in his halting and self-effacing fashion, people hung on his words. They expected and received insights into the way the steps of recovery work and into the way alcoholics think and act. Fred was concise, orderly, occasionally cerebral, but always instructive. He brought his years of experience as a theologian and teacher to his talks in A.A., but he never let that experience be obvious. No one ever got the feeling that they were in a classroom and Fred was instructing them. Rather, he shared just the way the other alcoholics shared, but the content of his talks seemed always to get to the bottom of things and to illustrate some important tool for living a sober and happy life.

Jim, on the other hand, was more spontaneous and less structured. His talks often seemed to start and end in the middle. When he began, there was no telling how long he would speak, but usually, especially in his early years, he spoke at length. The less serene would sometimes become impatient with him, especially at discussion meetings where each person present was given an opportunity to share, unless time for the meeting — usually ninety minutes — ran out. After a while, people began to realize that Jim had a much different approach than Fred. It was not so much the content of Jim's talks that drew people to him, it was the manner in which they were delivered. When Jim spoke, he was radiant. He was filled with joy and enthusiasm and gratitude. He was also absolutely certain that A.A. would work for him and for anybody who was listening, and he exhorted, cajoled, and reassured. His was a voice which penetrated despair and self-hatred.

"I ask God for the best and most," he was fond of saying. "The best I can be and the most I can do. And if the best and most I can do is get out of bed in the morning and feel sorry for myself, that's fine, as long as I get to a meeting. As long as I bring the body.

"'Bring the body,' my sponsor used to say, 'and the head will follow.' Oh, this poor sick head, how many times it has had to follow this poor sick body to a meeting. And all the way there it was saying, 'Oh poor Father Jim. Poor soul. Nobody understands. He's not like other people in A.A. If they had his problems, they'd feel sorry for themselves, too.' But I'd get to a meeting, and I'd listen, and I'd find out that I was exactly like other people in A.A. — full of self-pity, full of self-centeredness, and full of self-will. What a triple threat those are. This is such an exasperating disease. But we have a way out — a joyful way out. This is a joyful insanity. We are so blessed that God has brought us into this wonderful fellowship, that he loves us so much. Oh Jim, Jim, God loves you and he loves everybody here."

When he finished even the most severe doubters would admit the possibility of the truth of his statements, not because of compelling reasoning or rigorous logic, but because it was obvious to them that Jim believed what he was saying, that, in fact, he was enthralled by it all. If Fred was the apostle of action, Jim was the apostle of hope.

"Look out, Father," Kathleen screamed.

"For Christ's sake," Bobby yelled. "Forgive me. For crying out loud...."

The car shot forward.

"Oh my God," Kathleen shouted, "I am heartily sorry for having offended thee...."

"So am I," Bobby said. "Brake. Brake. Right there. Right in the middle. Brake. You can't miss it."

Jim peered under the steering wheel, and the car veered off the road and up on the grass.

"Help. Do something. Let me out. Help," Kathleen shouted.

Jim found the brake and jammed it toward the floor. The big Cadillac skidded on the lawn and came to a sudden stop with its front bumper resting gently on a large maple tree.

Bobby reached over and turned off the ignition, and they all sat in silence, Bobby and Father Jim in the front seat and Kathleen sprawled in the back with her eyes closed but her face tilted toward heaven.

"You know," Jim said after a moment, "I don't think I'm getting the hang of it."

Bobby looked at him with solemn disbelief.

"It looks so easy when you do it. You just jiggle this thing and turn this thing. But for me it's like trying to pat my head and rub my stomach at the same time."

The ash from his king-size Chesterfield fell on to the left leg of his new trousers, and he brushed it off onto the floor, leaving a grey smudge against the black.

Bobby sighed.

"I don't want to disappoint you," Jim said, "but I think that I have a very nervous disposition. I just don't think I have the kind of temperament it takes to learn how to drive."

"Really, Father. I mean, you know, it just takes a little practice. Doesn't it, Bobby?"

"For some people," Bobby said. "For others, it takes a bleeping miracle.

Jim emitted a short burst of laughter.

"You're really crude, you know that?" Kathleen said.

"You should hear what I think," Bobby answered.

Father Jim pondered the situation for a moment.

"I have always really liked taxicabs anyway," he said.

They formed the cadre — Kathleen, Bobby, and Anthony — but as time passed the circle widened. Kathleen's older sister came into the fellowship, and then her young nephew, Jerome, who Jim took a great liking to, and then friends of her family. People that Bobby had grown up with and drank with also came to A.A. And Anthony was the first of a whole crew of Lithuanians who came to meetings and got sober. There was a kind of geometric progression. As each of them got sober, friends and relatives who had trouble with alcohol noticed the improvement in their lives, and many of them, in turn, were attracted to A.A.

Jim was accepted by the staff at the state hospital. He even had his own keys to the locked wards. He ministered to the alcoholics and the non-alcoholics, to all who were broken and in need. The occasional new suit that he received from Bobby or from one of the alumni would become stained and tattered, the once white roman collar would yellow, and in the eyes of some of his fellow Jesuits, Jim would look like an eccentric Episcopalian or, indeed, like one of the inmates of the state hospital masquerading as a priest. But gradually, even those priests, the scholars and the teachers, the rugged, athletic, well-groomed Jesuits, were drawn to him. And it was Jim whom they sought out as a confessor. It was Jim who, when they were confused and disappointed or overworked or depressed or simply discouraged, reminded them and, indeed, sometimes made them aware for the first time at a very deep level that they were loved.

Even so, the members of his community had no idea of his work outside of the campus. He never talked about it, except with Fred, and Fred never spoke to anyone about his work or Jim's. So the two were often looked upon as drones. They were accepted and liked, but many of the other priests felt an unspoken superiority, as if Jim and Fred were not holding up their end.

Chapter Eight

As the years passed, there were times when Jim would disappear. No one in the fellowship would see him for a week or ten days. Then, finally, the word would leak out that he had been hospitalized again. And Jim's life would once more become crowded. The visitors would come and go all day long. Flowers would arrive, cards, baskets of fruit, all the things that convalescents receive. Jim, who was still bone thin, would give the baskets and the flowers away to nurses, custodians, and visitors, as soon as they were delivered, but the more he gave away, the more arrived. It was one of those paradoxes he enjoyed: No matter how many baskets of fruit and bouquets arrived, the room remained empty.

Jim suffered from a variety of ailments. His back was the chief culprit, but he also had poor circulation, touches of phlebitis, and respiratory problems. He had begun smoking long before cigarettes were known to be a health hazard. And now, he could not, for the life of him, give them up.

As much as he disliked being laid up, he always welcomed the first few days of a hospitalization. For one thing, whatever pain he was suffering usually abated, and, for another, he found peace and comfort and a chance to spend time with the two people he loved most in the world — Kathleen and Fred.

Over the years he had spent much time pondering both of those relationships and the very nature of friendship. He and Fred were so different in so many ways. Fred was logical, retiring, patient, deliberate, at times almost timid, at times humble almost to a fault, while Jim was often rash and frequently acted on the basis of half-formed ideas, acted intuitively rather than rationally — the way he used to bet the horses. Jim was gregarious and passionate and occasionally imperious. There was no better example of the difference between the two men than the time that Fred had been sick. They were in Boston, and Jim drove with him to an emergency ward of the city hospital. They were ignored for twenty minutes despite the fact that Fred was doubled over in pain. It was true that the waiting room was full and that many people seemed to be in pain. Fred counseled patience, but after a while his counsel fell on deaf ears, and Jim erupted. He demanded to see a doctor. When he was told to wait, he demanded to see the head administrator. When he was told to wait, he reached for the telephone and asked information for the telephone number of the Boston Herald. At once, the atmosphere changed. The personnel who had been officious were now conciliatory. Fred was taken into an examining room and within minutes he was rushed to an operating room. The doctors removed his appendix just as it was about to rupture.

"Your character defects saved my life," Fred told him later.

"And your virtues almost killed you," Jim answered.

Kathleen was another matter altogether. At first Jim had thought of her as a wounded bird. She was scrawny and flighty. She was, he had thought, essentially picaresque. But that was not so. She had been emotionally and spiritually maimed. Behind the facade of her disinterest and the 'you knows' of her disorderly mind was a vast, almost cosmic distress. Her uncertainty and her great capacity for self-destruction were for Jim indications of a far greater malady, a deep conviction on the part of Kathleen that she was unlovable. Jim was drawn to her as a healer is drawn to a cancer victim. And his constant response to her inadequacy and fear and desperation was love. But it was not a theoretical love or simply an act of the will, it was, at a very deep level, the response of one human to another's need and at the same time it expressed his need for another human being. Jim did not love Kathleen simply because she needed to be loved, he loved her also because he needed to love, and he loved her because there was an unspoken emotional and spiritual bond between them. He needed Kathleen as much as she needed him. They both needed to be loved.

He loved her in some ways as a father loves a daughter, but he also loved her as a friend and as a comrade, someone who understood rejection, defeat, sorrow, and hopelessness. And he loved her as men love women, not in a physical sense, for before everything else Jim was a priest and a celibate, but in that special interaction between the sexes that compliments the personalities and enhances moments with a mystery and vibrancy that simply does not exist between people of the same sex.

Kathleen. She was at once a mystery and a gift, a child and a friend, a mirror and yet, somehow, ineffable.

"The hordes are about to descend," she said looking

out the window at the parking lot. "Where do they all come from?"

"I don't know."

"I mean, how do you attract all these people? If I was in the hospital nobody would come to see me except you and Father Fred and my sister and my mother and my nephew and Bobby and Anthony.

"And maybe a couple of other people. Ten at most. Fifteen if it wasn't raining but it wasn't warm enough to go to the beach. You know?"

Father Jim did not answer.

"Although I guess that's something. I mean nobody ever came to visit me at the state hospital, except you," she said. She looked out at the sky, thinking back to those dark days.

"But you get sick, and the whole world beats a path to your door. I mean you got Jesuits coming up here. I mean they even come here to have you listen to their confession and I have to get out of the room. You even had that crazy bag lady come up here to visit you. Never mind all the flowers and the fruit. If you give me another basket of fruit I'm going to get terminal diarrhea. You know? Father, you know what I mean?"

"It's shameful that so many people could be so misled," Jim said.

"Never mind the fellow sufferers who drop in from the detox unit. I mean there are a whole — is a whole? — army of alkies who march in and out of here wearing slippers and bathrobes. And they all do that alky shuffle. You know? They're walking on their heels like the boat is rocking.

"And then there are the cab drivers. I mean from the Yellow Cab company. I mean, Father, really, cab drivers. And other people. Even normal people. I don't know where you find them."

"Neither do I," Jim said. "I guess water seeks its own level."

"Come on, Father. Get off it, will ya?"

"Off what?" Jim asked innocently.

"You're like the blipping pied piper. All these little rats go, 'Oops. There's Father Jim. Let's follow him.' It's like a parade."

Kathleen paused, thinking, still looking out the window.

"You can't give them all money? Can you?"

Jim laughed with delight.

Father Fred would come late at night after everyone else had gone home, and the two friends would sit, sometimes in lengthy conversations and sometimes in lengthy silences. Occasionally, it was a time for deep reflection.

"Sometimes I look back at it and I wonder," Jim said during one of these visits. "I wonder if I missed my calling, if the bus I was supposed to be on pulled out and I was left standing on the curb."

Fred listened in silence.

"All my friends are broken people. Even you, Fred, my best friend, are broken. You're not as broken as you were. Remember how your head used to shake?

"I thought that my friends would all be great minds, doers of great projects, that I would move in the circle of the elite. And here I am an old man with a broken body, addicted to cigarettes, and all of my friends are broken people. There isn't a great composer or a great writer or a great poet — at least that I know of — among them.

"You think of the great mystics. St. Teresa and John of the Cross. All the great saints who had such a personal and intimate relationship with Christ, and here I am getting only a glimpse now and then — just occasionally spotting his shadow a second after he turns the corner ahead of me.

"One night, years ago, as I was falling asleep, I heard his voice. I thought it was someone out in the hall. I can still remember it. 'Visit the sick. Comfort the afflicted. Heal the brokenhearted,' he said. And 'Follow me.' And I guess that's what we were doing when you went into the prisons and I went into the hospitals. Maybe you realized it, but I didn't. I just went. You suggested it. I wasn't even sure of what I was doing. Sometimes I wasn't even sure that he was with me. And I wound up receiving all these gifts, these wonderful broken people who turned out to be my friends. Kathleen, ah Fred, Kathleen. And Bobby with his impetuousness and his dreams of glory. And Anthony. Who would have expected Anthony to become such a power of example?

"And I think of what Peter asked him. 'What about us who have put aside everything to follow you?' And he said you will receive it back a hundredfold just in this life alone, never mind the one to come. And I have, Fred. I have received the hundredfold."

Jim closed his eyes and leaned back on his pillow.

"Kathleen asked me today where all these people come from — all the people who visit and send me candy and fruit and flowers. And I've been thinking about that. I don't know where they come from. I suppose that over the years I've gone to thousands of meetings and probably spoken thousands of times. We've been to Connecticut and Rhode Island and New Hampshire. We even went into Vermont and down past Stockbridge into New York. But why should people remember, and why should they care? Especially alcoholics. We're so self-centered. And me more than most. I don't know how you put up with me all these years. I talk and talk and talk and you listen and listen and listen. And you should be the one who talks and I should be the one who listens."

The two men fell silent until Fred was about to leave.

"You know, we are blessed," Jim said.

Fred nodded.

"I wonder what kind of man I would be if I was not an alcoholic. I wonder what kind of Jesuit. I'd probably be proud and off the track. I'd have wound up being an apostate or a ladies man. I would have been a disgrace to the Society. And instead, because I'm an alcoholic and because of A.A. and because of you, Fred, I have found love and peace and fulfillment. I have found friendship, and I have found my vocation even if it's not the one I expected."

Fred nodded.

"Good night, Jim."

"It's God that did it to us, Fred."

"I know."

PART THREE

Ascent to Jerusalem

Chapter One

*J*ack parked his car next to the yews which
bordered the long circular driveway and got
out. It was twilight and the white church
stood large and pure against the darkening summer sky.
A.A. is a place, he had been told, where Irish Catholics get
sober in the basements of Protestant churches. It was one
of those A.A. jokes he sort of liked and sort of loathed.
There was enough truth in it to make it funny but not
enough to make it sting. This meeting, for example, was
held in the church hall on the ground floor. It was true that
a lot of Irish Catholics would be in attendance, but there
would be a good representation of other ethnic groups,
French, Italian, Poles, Germans, here and there an American Indian, here and there a Jew.

Jack was jiggy. That too was an A.A. term. He could
not define it, but he knew what it meant. He was rattling

around inside. His palms were damp, and his mind kept leaping against the inside of his skull.

He knew the instant cure. It was a cure he had gone without for almost two months.

"Keep coming," they told him. "It gets better."

"When?" he had asked.

"Just keep coming. Don't drink and come to meetings," they said.

So he kept coming, kept waiting, kept hoping, and kept shaking. Others were coming too. Men and women — sometimes alone, sometimes in small groups — crossed the parking lot and walked up the driveway and entered the church hall. A few of them nodded to Jack, and he nodded back. It was all so strange. Most of them had spent their lives in bars. They were not the kind of people you would expect to find at a Congregational church. If they were the holier-than-thou, church guild types, he would have turned his back and gone to get the instant cure. But they weren't. They were like Jack. They were drunks. Some of them were lawyers, some of them were nuns, some of them were con men, and some of them were whores, and sometimes it was hard to tell who was who. He watched them go through the door, and then, for the fifty-seventh night in a row, he made a decision to join them.

Some groups had greeters who stood by the door. Some did not. This one did.

"Hi, my name's Mary. Welcome." She was in her late forties — tall, matronly. She did not look like a drunk. Jack shook her hand.

"I'm Will," a tall skinny man next to her said. "Welcome to our group."

"I'm Jack," he said. They shook hands and Jack was past the greeters and into the hall. It was loud and smokey.

Intermittently, a shrill female laugh would ride over the noise of the crowd. People were laughing, standing around in twos and threes. Jack was struck by the similarity to a cocktail party. He never felt comfortable at cocktail parties either. He never seemed to have anyone to talk to. It was embarrassing.

An outstretched hand was stuck in front of him.

"Hey, Jack, how are you?"

It was the short guy. Heavy. Always smiling. Always sticking his hand out. And Jack could never remember his name.

"I'm good. How you doing?"

"Good, good. You know, good," the shorter man said and was gone into the crowd.

Jack did not want the discomfort of standing by himself, so he quickly found a seat at the end of a row of metal chairs. An elderly priest was sitting at the other end of the row. Some ashes from his cigarette had fallen on his trouser leg. He gave Jack a huge smile as he dusted them off. Jack decided the priest must be an eccentric Episcopalian come to cheer the sinners on.

"Hi," the priest said, still smiling. "Good to see you."

Jack nodded and looked away. There was something vaguely familiar about him, and Jack wondered if they had ever drank together. But even so, he did not want to have a conversation with a skinny old man in the yellowed Roman collar who rubbed cigarette ashes into his black trousers. The old guy seemed so happy that Jack thought he might have a touch of senility. In fact, Jack began to wonder if he was really a clergyman or just some screw-ball who pretended to be a priest. Without meaning to or wanting to, Jack found himself keeping an eye on the man. There seemed to be a steady stream of people who wanted to talk to him. They came, one by one, coffee in hand, to sit next to him. They would say a few words, listen to something the priest said, and then get up and move away. Frequently, they would leave laughing or smiling. Some of them would walk away nodding their heads as if agreeing with something the priest had told them.

"What the hell is going on here?" Jack wondered. "What is that old guy saying to them? Why are they laughing? What the hell could be so funny?"

To Jack's eyes, the priest was decrepit beyond belief. There was no telling how old he was. Even sitting down, he was hunched over.

His shoulders were rounded and he looked like he had curvature of the spine. His long white fingers were stained with nicotine, and he was so thin that he bordered on being emaciated. His black suit was so tattered and frayed that it looked like it belonged to a hobo. And yet he was smiling, and his smile seemed to transform others. There was something maddening about it. What did these people see in this old, maybe senile, priest that he could not see?

Jack went to seek refuge in the coffee line.

"You been around long?" a man behind him asked.

Jack turned. "Me?" He looked the man over. Crisply pressed slacks, jacket, tie, and shoes with a sparkling shine.

"Yeah, you," the man said. Jack caught the smell of fresh alcohol on the man's breath.

"Fifty-seven days."

"Fifty-seven days? Christ. How d'you do it?"

Jack saw that he wasn't being ironic.

"They told me not to drink even if my ass fell off," Jack said.

The man laughed. "Did it fall off?"

"Not yet."

"Fifty-seven days. Fifty-seven days," the man repeated. Jack started to feel a little like an old-timer.

"Good evening everybody," a voice said over the loud-speaker. "Good evening everybody." Gradually the roar of voices ebbed.

"My name is Jeff, and I'm an alcoholic, and this is the regular Wednesday night meeting of the Joy of Living Group of Alcoholics Anonymous. I'd like to start this meeting as we start all meetings in A.A. with a moment of silence to do with as you wish."

The hall was suddenly hushed. People stopped pouring coffee. Here and there a head was bent.

Jeff reached into his back pocket, pulled out his wallet and took a card from it.

"I'll read the Preamble: 'Alcoholics Anonymous is a fellowship of men and women who share their experience, strength and hope with each other that they may solve their common problem and help others to recover from alcoholism. The only requirement for membership is a desire to stop drinking. There are no dues or fees for A.A. membership; we are self-supporting through our own con-tributions. A.A. is not allied with any sect, denomination, politics, organization or institution; does not wish to engage in any controversy; neither endorses nor opposes any causes. Our primary purpose is to stay sober and help other alcoholics to achieve sobriety.' "

Jeff paused. He put the card back in his wallet and his wallet back in his pocket.

"As I said, I'm Jeff and I'm an alcoholic. I want to wel-come you to the Joy of Living Group. If this is your first meeting or one of your first meetings, relax. You're among friends. If you think you may be having a problem with booze, you're in the right place. Try to listen to what the speakers say. And try to do what we do — identify and not compare. Comparing is when you say, 'I never did that,' or 'I'm not that bad yet,' or 'When I get that bad, I'll do something about my drinking.' When we identify, we see that the same thing or something like it has happened to us or could happen to us, or we can identify with the feelings of the speaker — fear or anxiety or grandiosity.

"I've never been a mother," Jeff said. There were a few snickers, and Jeff smiled. "But I can identify with mothers who drank and who had trouble with it, because I drank, and I had trouble with it, and that's why I'm here. I'm here to learn how to go one day without one drink. And I learn it from you people because there are an awful lot of people who are going one day without one drink. If you're new and you want what we've got, then try to listen. Sometimes you hear people say, 'Take the cotton out of your ears and stick it in your mouth,' and there's something to that."

Jack got his coffee and went back to his seat. He still did not know how this thing worked. There weren't any psychiatrists, no social workers, no nurses running around with charts. He had been to meetings for more than eight weeks, and he had yet to hear a medical discussion of alcoholism, and so far no one had mentioned the superego or the unconscious. Had he been a snob, he might have been appalled. The men and women who spoke didn't seem to have any special scientific knowledge. They freely admitted that they did not know much about the mechanics of the disease of alcoholism. But they had something. Jack recognized that. He just did not recognize what it was that they had.

Jack put the styrofoam cup on the floor between his feet and surveyed the hall. Most of the halls he had been to were much older. They had bad lighting, dark colored walls, old fashioned plumbing, dirty floors. This hall was different; it sparkled.

"The Joy of Living Group is putting on its own meeting tonight," Jeff said. He scanned the audience until his eyes lighted on a woman in her mid-thirties. "And Sally is going to chair," he said.

There was polite applause, welcoming and not prolonged. Sally moved to the microphone and put her cup of coffee down on the card table next to it. She put a long cigarette to her lips, lit it, and inhaled deeply.

"Hi everybody. I'm Sally, and I'm a nervous alcoholic," she said. "Did we have the moment of silence?" Heads nodded. "Did Jeff read the Pre-amble?" More nods. "Oh Jeff, you're so efficient." There was laughter. "Well, you know, the chairperson chairs and the speakers speak, so I'm not going to say much. I'll say a little to qualify myself as an alcoholic, and then I'll sit down and call my speakers."

She took another deep drag on her cigarette. She was a pretty woman with sandy hair. She wore a print blouse with a flower design and a light green skirt. She seemed to Jack to be well-tailored without being ostentatious.

"Oh, I don't know where to start tonight. When Jeff asked me to chair the meeting, I wanted to say 'no.' But I try never to say 'no' in A.A. So here I am folks, and I hope you'll bear with me."

She took another deep pull on her cigarette and exhaled.

"I'm one of those mothers Jeff was talking about. I always wanted to be a mother. Some kids want to grow up to be movie stars or nurses or teachers. I wanted to be a mother. I wanted to be the perfect mother. Not like my own mother. Different. The perfect wife, with the perfect house, with the perfect lawn. And I wound up living in a pig sty. I couldn't take care of the kids. I couldn't feed my husband. I couldn't even take a bath."

She fluffed her hair.

"This was like dirty straw. I wore the same house dress for six months. My God, I think they had to cut it off me." Everybody laughed, including the priest. Jack smiled. "I would sit in my living room. The kids were at school and my husband was at work, and I'd have my vodka bottle next to me. You know. Sort of hidden by the side of the chair. Just in case President Nixon or Princess Margaret came to visit. I wouldn't want them to think I was drinking at ten o'clock in the morning. They might not understand. I mean, I understood. If they had my problems, they'd be drinking at ten o'clock in the morning too. That's what I thought. Can you imagine? There I was, the perfect mother and the perfect wife, in a house dress that was so dirty it was stiff. I couldn't answer the telephone. I couldn't answer the door. All the shades were drawn. I hadn't been outside the house in two months. Nobody came to see me. Nobody wanted to see me. Everybody thought I was nuts. I don't know how my husband stood it. There I was drinking around the clock in that raunchy old house dress, and I was hiding the vodka bottle just in case the President walked into the room."

She did not look nervous anymore. It was a big hall. There were almost three hundred people listening to her, but Sally was talking as if she were back in her living room chatting with friends.

"Insane. That's what it was. Absolute insanity. The perfect mother had become a drunk. I turned my living room into skid row. I shouldn't say nobody came to visit me. I had one friend left, and she used to come to see me. She knew I was an alcoholic, and she knew about A.A. 'Sally,' she used to say, 'don't you think you're having a problem with booze?' Are you kidding? Me? I wasn't having a problem with booze. I was having a problem with my living room. It was so depressing. If we lived someplace else, I wouldn't have been depressed. And that husband of mine. That bastard. Can you imagine? He expected to have his food on the table when he got home from work. How did he think I could make him his dinner when I had to sit there all day and be depressed by that goddamn living room?"

The laughter was frequent and warm now, and Jack all but forgot about the old priest sitting a few seats away from him. This woman was alive; she was vibrant. He had never been a mother either, but he knew what she was talking about.

"That's what alcohol did to me. It turned everything around. It made it impossible for me to have the things I wanted most in life. It turned me into a zombie. Maybe you're sitting there saying to yourself that you only drink in lounges and you're not that bad. Well, let me tell you, honey, if you're an alcoholic and you continue to drink, all the 'yets' that haven't happened yet will happen. Some people come here and they hear horror stories, and they say to themselves, 'That couldn't happen to me. I'll never get that bad,' or 'When I get that bad I'll do something about my drinking.' And they go back out there and all the things that haven't happened to them yet, happen. And some of them never make it back here. They die or they go to the nut house or they go to jail. Those are the three places you can go if you continue to drink. Or you can come here and you can get better. It's up to you. The door swings both ways in A.A. But that's enough out of me for a while. I think I'm going to call my first speaker. Father Jim."

Again there was applause. But this time it was raucous. There were cheers and whistles. Jack had never heard anything like it at an A.A. meeting. It sounded like a ball park. It sounded like Babe Ruth was coming to bat.

The old priest stood up slowly with the help of his cane. Jack saw him out of the corner of his eye, and noticed that the cuffs on his black suit coat were frayed. At first he thought the priest was going for a cup of coffee or perhaps to the men's room. But instead of going to the rear of the hall, the priest walked, slightly stooped, to the microphone, all the while with a huge smile on his face.

"Thanks. I'm Father Jim, and I'm an alcoholic. And I'm grateful to be here with my friends tonight."

He stopped for a moment and looked around the hall, as if trying to spot familiar faces, before continuing.

"It's important for me to come to meetings and hear the speakers. My sponsor used to say to me, 'Jim, if you can only get to a meeting for five minutes, then go for the five minutes. You'll hear what you need to hear.' And many times I have only been able to get to a meeting for a few minutes, and it would just happen to be the right few minutes. The speaker would talk about something that I needed to hear that day to save my life."

Again he paused, this time as if to gather his thoughts.

"This is a powerful, baffling, and insidious disease that we have. I remember when I was first getting sober, I would be filled with self pity, and despair. 'Oh, poor Father Jim,' I used to think, 'Nobody understands.' And sometimes I would become so discouraged or so angry that I'd start to swear. You know, I never used to swear before I came to A.A. So one day, I went to my sponsor, Rip, and I said, 'I'm swearing like a marine.' 'Jim,' he told me, 'This disease would make a saint swear.'

"You see, I misread the second step. It says that we came to believe that a power greater than ourselves could restore us to sanity. I thought it said, 'restore us to sanctity.' That's why Rip used to make me write out the steps. When we get here, we're sick. Our brains don't work as

well as we think they do. Our emotions are raw and
swollen out of proportion to the rest of us. And we have to
listen to the people who have been sober for a while
because they know how it's done. And we have to make
haste slowly."

Jim laughed at the paradox and slowly surveyed his
audience again.

"It starts off very innocently for a lot of us. In fact,
some of us don't even remember when we had our first
drink. That's why this disease is so cunning. It sneaks up
on us and traps us before we know what happened. I did-
n't start to drink until I became a Jesuit. And then I was
the life of the party. When we would have our affairs, I'd
always make the drinks, and some of the other young
Jesuits would come to me and say, 'Jim, we wish we could
drink like you.' They wanted me to teach them how to
drink."

He let the irony hang in the air for just a moment.

"After a while I started to buy bottles for myself. But
when I went into a package store, I'd pretend I was a
parish priest and that I didn't know anything about booze.
I'd tell them it was for my pastor, that I wanted a bottle of
something or other for my poor old pastor who wasn't
feeling too well, and what would they suggest. Then I'd
sneak the bottle back to my room.

"My problem was not just alcohol. I've had a bad back
since I was in high school. I have lots of pain and I've had
a number of operations. Doctors who were trying to help
me prescribed drugs so that I could sleep and drugs to
take away the pain. But I took so much medication that
towards the end, the pills had reverse effects. Uppers
would put me to sleep, and downers would wake me up.
I'd walk around with a big bottle of uppers in my right
pocket and a big bottle of sleeping pills in my left pocket.

I'd take the sleeping pills to wake up and the uppers to get to sleep."

Father Jim smiled. It was a big, broad smile, an all encompassing smile. It was the smile of youth and wonder and adventure, and Jack who had difficulty smiling himself began to be charmed by the man.

"I ended up in the hospital in the psychiatric unit. I was in a depression so deep that I couldn't speak from January until May. I didn't even recognize my own mother when she came to visit me. She had been so proud of me. She used to refer to me as 'Father Jim' to her friends. 'Father Jim did this or Father Jim did that.' She always kept a room ready at home so that Father Jim could visit. But in the end, my mother had to tell me that I was no longer welcome at home. This disease will take everything from us, everything that we love most, everyone that we love most.

"Father Fred used to come to visit me every day and try to get me to talk. I didn't know him either. He used to ask the nurse if his coming to see me did any good, and she'd tell him to keep coming. They thought I was hopeless, that I had lost everything. Lost the priesthood. Month after month, I just sat there.

"I loved music. I loved literature and I loved sports. I even loved the horses. But I lost all of that — and I also lost my Mass. I couldn't say it. I was so, so sick. But you know there are people in state hospitals who aren't as sick as we were who will never get out."

Father Jim looked back at the eyes that were fixed on him. He was stooped and gray, but there was an air of youth and joyful innocence about him. It was difficult to imagine him as an active alcoholic — he was so full of life, so eager to share his thoughts. His enthusiasm was magnetic.

"We're so sick and so full of pride when we get here. When I came into A.A. I was a bag of bones. I hadn't done anything right in years. I thought I knew everything. But I really didn't know anything at all. I remember one time I was telling Rip about all the physical problems I had, and how I drank to ease the pain and to let me sleep, and I asked him if he thought I was really an alcoholic. 'Father Jim,' he said, 'If you're not, you'll sure do until the real thing comes along.' "

The hall erupted with laughter, and Jim laughed along with his audience.

"I'll do until the real thing comes along," he said.

"What an insidious disease this is. We are so sick, and we refuse to admit it. But if we want to get better we have to admit that we're powerless over alcohol. I had to admit a lot of other things too. I'm a priest, and I had to admit that I didn't know how to pray. When I first started to go to meetings, people would say to me, 'Oh, Father Jim, you're a priest. You know all about the spiritual side of the program.' And of course I'd agree with them. I didn't know what they were talking about, but I'd agree with them. Finally, a garbage man from Detroit told me I didn't know how to pray. And then he taught me."

He nodded his head as if in confirmation of his own words.

"Pride. It's so important to us. Our dignity. Rip used to tell me to ask for help as soon as I got out of bed in the morning. And I was hurt.

" 'Rip, I say my morning prayers in the chapel.' "

He looked very meek, and his voice imitated that of a whining child.

"And he asked, 'Father, Jim, did you ever pick up a drink on the way to the chapel?' "

Father Jim's eyes went heavenward.

"Yes, Rip," he said in the child's voice.

Again there was laughter as Jim looked like an adolescent who had just been corrected.

"So he told me to put my shoes under the bed when I went to sleep at night, and in the morning, while I was down on my knees trying to get them, to ask for help. And you know, that's the beginning — asking for help, asking God to do for us what we can't do for ourselves. Every day, I ask God to keep me away from a drink and a pill, and every night I thank him. That's been going on for eighteen years now. Every morning and every night.

"Sometimes I get into bed at night and I have so much pain from my back that I think I will never get to sleep. And then I ask God for the gift of sleep, and the next thing I know it's morning."

He took a deep breath, and Jack realized that he did not want the old priest to stop speaking.

"We learn a lot of things in A.A. — things that we might never have learned if we didn't come here. We learn that pride is our enemy and humility is our friend. You know, when I first came back to the city after spending so much time at Guest House, I was afraid to go to meetings. I was afraid of what the other Jesuits would think. I was afraid that they would think that I was a spiritual cripple. Father Fred tried to talk to me — in fact he was very worried about me — but I wouldn't listen. And for three days, I pretty much stayed in my room — just the way I did when I was drinking. I was hiding out, and I didn't realize it.

"And then, without thinking about it, I began to say the Serenity Prayer. 'God grant me the serenity to accept the things I cannot change. Courage to change the things I can. And wisdom to know the difference.' I couldn't change the fact that I'm an alcoholic and I need meetings to stay sober. And I needed courage to come out of my room and start my A.A. life in the city. And I got what I needed.

"And you know, I later met a woman in A.A. who had brain damage from drinking. And all she could remember from that prayer was 'wisdom to know the difference.' So when she prayed she said, 'God give me the wisdom to know the difference.' And it worked for her. She stayed sober.

"So we have to make the effort, whatever effort we can. And God will do the rest."

Father Jim was silent for a long moment.

"You know, I had a blueprint for my life. I carried it around in the back of my skull. I thought it was the perfect design for Father Jim. I would teach. And occasionally I would go across the country giving lectures, the way I used to.

"But that was not God's plan for me. He wanted me to stay here in this city with my A.A. friends. And that's what I have done. And I found that God's plan was better than mine. I have found a joy and a peace that I never knew existed. I have been freed from darkness and insanity and the prison of self. I love and I am loved, and it's a wonderful life.

"When we come to A.A., we shake and we spill coffee and we can't sleep. We're nervous wrecks. We think we're going to jump out of our skins. Everybody around us is laughing and talking and having a wonderful time, and we're falling apart. Oh, it all seems so black. But it's not. Behind the pain and confusion there is a ray of hope. For a lot of us, it's the first time we have even heard a whisper of hope. But it's there and it's the promise of a new life."

He paused, and Jack thought that he had finished speaking, but he leaned forward and spoke another sentence into the microphone.

"God did not rescue you from alcohol so that you could go insane or commit suicide."

It was like a thunderbolt. At least for Jack. He did not know why, but the sentence pierced his anxiety and his fear. It riveted him.

Even though he and Father Jim were not acquainted, and even though there were hundreds of other people in the hall, Jack knew that the remark was directed specifically at him.

"God rescued me?" he thought. "Is that possible?"

There was prolonged applause. When it was over, Sally came to the microphone and announced that they would take a break and have a raffle for the Big Book.

But Jack continued to ponder that sentence.

"God," he thought, "the God of 'Let there be light and there was light' — that God — rescued me?"

It was impossible. It was asinine. It was inconceivable. But it was true.

Jack remembered now what had gotten him into A.A. He had been drunk — in a blackout — lying face down on the floor. He came out of it long enough to lift his face toward the ceiling.

"God. I can't go on like this any longer. Please give me the answer." That was all he said. It did not even seem like a prayer. He had tried everything else. Psychiatry. Psychology. Self-help books. Exercise. Nothing had worked. He slipped back into the blackout, and when he woke up the next morning he had forgotten about the prayer. He was falling apart, and he called a psychiatrist for tranquilizers. The doctor refused to prescribe them. Instead, he suggested that Jack call A.A. And Jack, who had no idea that alcohol was his problem, made the telephone call. When he did, the veil was lifted from his eyes, he understood that booze — which he thought was keeping him from going insane — was in fact destroying him. Since then he had been going to meetings and not drinking for fifty-seven days.

It was only when Father Jim used the term 'rescue' that Jack remembered his prayer, and he came to believe that there was a causal relationship between his drunken plea and his sobriety.

The hum of conversation returned as people bought tickets for the raffle. Many in the audience left their seats and went to the coffee line. Jack sat where he was. He watched Father Jim shaking hands and smiling as he worked his way back toward his seat. And he recognized a strength in the old man that was masked by his frailty and by his manner. It was a strength that Jack knew he himself did not possess.

He continued to ponder the priest's words. Since he had stopped drinking, he had two great fears. One was that he would go insane. The other was that he would commit suicide. Now, Father Jim had introduced him to a revolutionary concept. If God did rescue him from alcohol — as impossible as that seemed — and if it wasn't so that he could go insane or commit suicide, perhaps God had something else in mind. Could it be that God wanted him to get well? Was that possible? That a supreme being actual cared about what happened to him? That God would take the extraordinary action of managing to get him to A.A.? It seemed almost ridiculous, and yet, it seemed that that is exactly what had happened.

Jack did not hear the other speakers. He stayed for a while after the meeting ended. But his mind continued to dwell on Father Jim's words, and he hardly noticed the people who milled around chatting and drinking coffee.

When he left the church, he had to walk around a crowd of people who were gathered on the side walk. He paid no attention to them, and he hardly noticed the ambulance which came racing up the hill with its siren wailing and its life flashing.

For the first time, Jack began to suspect that he could get better. And that revelation blocked out everything else.

Chapter Two

He was back in St. Vincent Hospital. Wednesday night, after he had spoken at the meeting, he collapsed as he was leaving the church hall. An ambulance had rushed to the scene, its siren wailing. It came up the driveway to within a few feet of where Father Jim lay, his head propped up by a suit jacket that had been turned into a makeshift pillow. A man and a woman, both dressed in blue with American flag patches sewn onto the tops of their sleeves, leapt out of the ambulance and quickly wheeled a stretcher next to the priest. They were surprised at how light he was as they moved him from the macadam to the stretcher. One of them could have handled him without any trouble. It only took a few moments and the ambulance was gone, flashing lights disappearing down the hill. Its siren could be heard for another minute or so and then that too was gone.

He had left the hospital only a few weeks earlier. Now he was lying emaciated and ashen on a bed which seemed to swallow his frail figure. At first they thought it was a heart attack, then they thought it was gastritis, then they thought that it was malnutrition and dehydration. He seemed to rally once they began to feed him intravenously. His color began to come back, and now and then he managed a smile. After a few days, they were able to get him up and walk him down the corridor. And after a week they began to talk of sending him home. It seemed like just another tribulation in the long string of tribulations that Jim had suffered. But Fred intuitively recognized that this time something was different. Jim was not himself. Despite his obvious efforts, there were times when he could not contain his irritability. He was like an athlete before a big game. His focus had narrowed to the coming contest. He did not speak about it. Perhaps he did not even think about it. Still, he was consumed by it.

Fred sat with Jim the day before he was to leave the hospital. Their conversation was sporadic and haphazard. They would pick up the thread of a thought for a moment and then drop it into the silence of the sunlit room. They had spoken so often and explored so much that they could speak in bits and pieces, building a dialogue on fragments.

A nurse broke into their silence to take Jim's blood pressure. His reaction was sharp, unforeseen, and atypical.

"Can't you see I'm speaking with my spiritual father?" he asked, his voice irritable and edged with anger.

The nurse left the room without a word.

"They never leave you alone," he said. "They spend your whole life waking you up and sticking needles in you. 'Open. Close. Breathe. Don't Breathe. Roll over.' They act as if you're a pet collie."

Fred said nothing. They both knew what the dying

were like. And although death seemed nowhere on the horizon, they both knew he was lurking outside the room, ready to pounce on Jim and engage him in the final battle.

"If it be not now, yet it will come. The readiness is all," Fred thought.

"Down to this. After all these years," Jim said, as if reading that thought.

Fred left before the onset of the final agony. Jim was alone in the room, and he got up from the bed to walk to the window. In an instant, he was falling to the floor, and he knew why they called it a 'shock.' It felt like that, as if someone had stabbed his brain with an electrical charge. His eyes focused so sharply that he thought he could see the molecules in the glass window. He heard the groan come out of him and felt the overwhelming surge of pain, and as he fell to the floor and consciousness spun away from him, he knew that his last struggle had begun.

Fred called Kathleen's home as soon as he received word from the hospital, and when Kathleen got the message, she went immediately to see Father Jim, but she went with no foreboding. In the fifteen years she had known Jim, she had seen him in the hospital many times. Jim was sickly. It was part of his nature. So she came to his room expecting that the doctors had exaggerated the seriousness of his condition.

The soft June twilight was turning to darkness when Kathleen arrived at the hospital. Visiting hours were ending and she waited for about fifteen people to get off the elevator before she could get on. She rode alone to the fifth floor, and walked quickly to Father Jim's room without stopping at the nurses' station. The door was three-quarters closed and an 'Oxygen in Use — No Smoking Sign' hung from it. As Kathleen pushed through the door, she tried to think of a joke which would put the situation in perspective. But one look at the bed told her that it was not a time for joking.

Jim was shrunken and ghostly in the dimness. His eyes were closed, and his breathing was slow and labored. An intravenous bottle hung next to the bed and a tube extended down to his arm. There was a plastic hose which circled his cheeks and led to his nostrils. His lips were parched and cracked.

Kathleen worked in a nursing home, and she was familiar with the signs of death. She looked down at Jim's hand and saw that his fingernails were turning blue. She took his hand in hers and slowly bent to kiss it. Suddenly Father Jim lunged up. He hugged her very tightly.

"I love you, Father Jim," Kathleen said. She noticed that she was crying. "I want you to know how much I love you. I want you to know that."

She was surprised by the thinness of his arm. But she was even more surprised by his strength. For just a moment, it gave her hope.

Without uttering a word, Father Jim relaxed and he sank back on the bed. Kathleen could not tell if he was conscious — whether he was even aware that he had hugged her or if the action had just been a reflex.

She did not admit it to herself, but she understood that the death watch had begun. The others arrived within minutes — Fred, Bobby and her nephew Jerome. They were the nucleus. There were others who came and went. Some stood out in the hall smoking and speaking in whispers, others would linger in the corner of Father Jim's room quietly praying.

Jerome did not pray much. Mostly he watched. He was seventeen years old, and he had been in A.A. for three years. He was a freshman in high school, strung out on pills and drinking whenever he could, when he went to his aunt and asked her for help. Kathleen had introduced him to Jim and the old man and the fourteen year old boy had become friends. Jerome did not reflect on the friendship until that night standing in the shadows of the hospital room. He and the old priest had something in common, something besides being alcoholic, something that had provided a foundation for their friendship. It was, Jerome thought now, that they had similar outlooks — that in many respects Father Jim was a teenager, and that in some respects, Jerome was an old man.

At first, Jerome felt awkward, watching as nurses bustled past him and old friends peeked through the door and waved to Father Fred, but that feeling quickly passed and he realized that no one was paying attention to him or, indeed, was even aware of his presence. So Jerome became like a silent camera. He had never been present at such a dramatic scene, and he was filled with a sense of excitement. Father Jim did not seem like Father Jim at all. He lay in the bed unconscious, sometimes peaceful, sometimes thrashing about. It was only when he moaned that his agony became a momentary reality and Jerome would identify the frail body with his friend.

A number of priests came and went. Jerome had seen some of them walking around the campus. They seemed to lack the awe for death that most of the others had. They spoke in normal tones without whispering. Some of them even smiled.

"You'll be with Jesus soon, Jim," one of them had almost shouted in Jim's ear. "Not too long now, Jim. You'll get there ahead of us. Put in a good word for me."

Were they joking, Jerome wondered, at such a serious time?

At that moment there was a violent spasm in Jim's body. His arms and legs jerked, and a short sharp groan burst from his throat. He became deathly still for a moment, and Jerome thought that perhaps he had died, but then his entire body began to twitch. It was like an aftershock which follows an earthquake, Jerome thought.

Kathleen took a small damp towel and wiped Father Jim's forehead and cheeks. His eyes remained closed, but the twitching stopped.

It was, Jerome thought, as if a play was being staged in the room and each person had assumed the role of an actor. Here was a drama developing its own rhythm and its own cast of characters. Kathleen was now something more than Kathleen. She was nurse, daughter, attendant — a major character at center stage. Father Fred, too, had assumed another role. He was the friend, brother, consoler, and mentor. When permission was needed for anything, it was Father Fred who granted it, and it was Father Fred who, at about ten o'clock, led them in a rosary. Jerome hardly prayed. He hugged the corner and watched the dangling beads sway and the faces concentrated in prayer.

Something else was going on too, but Jerome could not at first grasp what it was. Then as he listened to the Hail Marys and stared at Father Jim's stiff body and the faces that surrounded the bed, it seemed as if the entire drama was now focused on the frail and dying priest. His bed was both a stage and an altar — a place of battle and a place of sacrifice. And Father Jim, himself, was at once warrior, prize, and sacrificial victim. Jerome half expected death to come through the doorway and attempt to drag Father Jim from the room. In his imagination, Jerome saw Father Fred lift the crucifix from his rosary and drive death from the room the way the hero uses a cross to drive Dracula away in the movies.

Outside, people were driving cars, watching television, drinking in bars, going to bed — unaware of the great contest taking place in the hospital room —a contest that every one of them, including himself, would have to engage in. It cried out for poetry, for great words in noble speeches, but instead the responses were mostly inarticulate. There were nods and gestures and heads bent in prayer. Something mysterious was going on, something awe-inspiring, and they were inarticulate witnesses, unable to grasp its power or to really understand its majesty.

Cheryl burst through the door, looking as if she thought she might have come too late. Jerome, detached and unnoticed, studied her without realizing he was studying her. She was nervous, excited, but obviously on a mission. Jerome knew her slightly. She was a friend mainly of Father Fred's, but Jerome knew from listening to Kathleen that Father Jim had kept her from committing suicide.

"I just heard," she said to Fred. "I came to consecrate him."

Jerome did not know what she meant, but apparently Fred did. "Consecrate?" Kathleen asked.

Fred did not answer either of the women. He looked down at Jim. It was impossible to tell how near the end was. It could be minutes, hours, even a day or two.

"What does she mean, Father?" Kathleen was insistent.

Fred answered her so softly that Jerome could not hear what he was saying, but Kathleen looked at Cheryl and then nodded as if in agreement.

Suddenly a great anguish came over the unconscious priest. Pained and mournful groans filled the room, and his arms and legs thrashed sporadically in short whip-like movements.

Jerome looked at his friend and saw his pain but did not feel it. Father Jim was alone, even with friends around him, detached from them, engaged in a mysterious conflict that involved his very being. They could not help him. They could not even really grasp what was happening. They could only watch.

"Virgin of Fatima," Jerome heard Father Fred say. "Refuge of sinners."

Jerome focused his entire attention on Fred and strained to hear his words, but Fred was speaking softly and Jim was groaning and thrashing.

"We consecrate..."

There was a full and terrible moan from Jim.

"To your Immaculate Heart."

Jerome looked at Father Jim. The veins protruded from his neck. He seemed to be straining for something.

"...entrust...our priesthood...in this hour of decision that weighs upon the world...."

Jim stopped thrashing and his body relaxed. His breathing became regular and a great stillness came over the room.

"She's here," Cheryl whispered.

Jerome looked but he saw nothing.

"She's here," Cheryl said again.

Fred nodded.

"Who's here?" Jerome wondered. He wanted to call over to Cheryl. "Who's here?" But he didn't. He clung to the shadows. He wanted to observe all of it. To be there.

After a half hour had passed Kathleen and Bobby decided to go out for a sandwich. They asked Jerome to come with them, but he would not leave his corner of the room. He had been standing in silence for more than two hours. Mostly his eyes were on Jim, as if by observing he could understand. Before she left, Kathleen took a chair from near the bed and slid it across to the corner so that Jerome could sit down.

Jerome was aware that the vigil had now been reduced to two. Cheryl had gone out into the hall to talk with two or three people from A.A. Father Fred sat next to the bed. His eyes were closed and rosary beads hung from his right hand. Occasionally his lips would move. But most of the time his face was rigid and impassive. Jerome did not pray, he did not even think. He was aware of the sounds. Now and then he could hear a cough or a raised voice from the corridor. There was a soft steady hum in the room, but he did not know its source. Father Jim's breathing was steady but shallow. It had the regularity of a second hand, except that every couple of minutes it would stop for what seemed to be a very long time. And then it would resume.

At about midnight, Father Jim's right forearm began to flop against the sheets. It reminded Jerome of a fish flopping on the bottom of a rowboat. Fred did not move. He kept his eyes closed, but Jerome could see from the look on his face that his praying had become more intense.

A groan, deep and sounding like it came from another world, filled the room.

Jerome leaned forward in his chair.

There was another groan. This time it was thin and throaty.

A tremor went though Father Jim's body.

Jerome found himself standing and moving toward the bed.

Father Jim's eyes opened.

"Kathleen," he cried. His voice was loud, mournful.

Jerome took his hand. It was cold and stiff. It felt almost like cardboard.

Father Fred was also standing.

"Into your hands, Lord, I commend my spirit," Fred said.

A long low sound escaped from Father Jim's throat. His eyes were open but unfocused. The sound stopped and Jim's jaw sagged toward his chest.

Cheryl had come back in the room. She was standing at the foot of the bed.

The three of them stared at the perfectly still Father Jim.

Finally, Father Fred broke the silence.

"Eternal rest grant to him, O Lord. May perpetual light shine upon him, and may his soul and the souls of all the faithful departed through the mercy of Christ rest in peace," he said.

They stood there for another few moments before calling a nurse.

Death had come so quickly that it had eluded Jerome's attempt to grasp and comprehend it.

Father Jim had left the room and only his body and the mystery of it all remained.

When Kathleen and Bobby returned at about twelve forty-five, the main doors of the hospital were locked. They saw a janitor inside, and they banged on the glass until he came and opened the door.

"We're going up to Father Jim Collins' room," Kathleen told the man.

"Oh, Father Collins. Yeah. They just brought his body downstairs," the janitor said.

Kathleen looked at him in disbelief. "We're going up to the room anyway," she said.

The room was empty when they got to it. All that remained was a vase of flowers that someone had sent to Father Jim. Kathleen took the flowers — to the consternation of a nurse's aid. Kathleen did not care what the woman thought. She wanted something that had been Father Jim's, and only the flowers were left.

Chapter Three

It was a perfect June day. The sky was a vast blue with only a wisp of cloud near the horizon. In another hour, as the sun began to set, that wisp would change to orange and then to red. As Doctor Collins turned his car into the main gate of Holy Cross, he saw that the subtle shift from late spring to summer had taken place without his noticing. The trees that lined the drive were full-leaved and stately, and they enhanced the air of regal dignity and permanence that he associated with the college. The campus had changed a great deal since he and Jim had been students a half-century earlier, but the old buildings were still there, and he felt a wave of nostalgia as he drove slowly past the library and around the Hall. His wife and son were also in the car, but they too were silent.

Doctor Collins had been to Jesuit funerals before. They were quiet affairs, especially when school was out. A wake at the college was a far cry from a wake in his home town. At home, a good wake was a social occasion. Relatives and old friends gossiped and reminisced. They noted the passing of the years and called the roll of the dead. All who were able came. Not many people showed up for a Jesuit wake — a handful of family, other priests, maybe a few students, and that was it. He hoped that one or two of his classmates would turn out, but he doubted that they would. They were scattered around the country. A number of them had died. The wake would be quiet, an occasional visitor, some sporadic conversation, and then some coffee or a drink afterward. A drink — he still felt embarrassed about Jim's drinking even though he knew it had been more than fifteen years since Jim had tied one on, but he was confident that no one would broach the subject. After all, it was a wake. Perhaps it was just as well that it would be a quiet affair, given Jim's history. But still, it did not seem quite fair. After all, Jim had dedicated his life to a noble cause, even if it had not worked out too well, at least the intention had been there.

Jim would be laid out at Loyola Hall, the priests' residence toward the rear of the campus, and he would be buried from the small chapel that was located in the hall for the use of the priests. It was too bad that he could not be buried from St. Joseph's — the campus chapel — Doctor Collins thought. Despite its name, the campus chapel was really a good-sized church — but only the important Jesuits were buried from there. The priests' private chapel in Loyola Hall was more than big enough for the rest of them. Too bad. Jim had had great potential. Several of his classmates had risen to great prominence. It was a shame that Jim had had so much to contend with.

The rector, Father Rafferty, and several other priests were on hand to greet the Collinses when they entered Loyola.

"Doctor Collins, good to see you," Father Rafferty said. "Sorry about Jim. A good man."

"Thanks. You know my wife, May, and my son, Dermot."

"Yes, of course. Hello, Mrs. Collins. Hello, Dermot. Why don't we go in and see Jim? It's getting close to seven, and others will be coming, I'm sure."

Jim was laid out in white altar vestments which were bordered with green. He looked very ancient and very peaceful. Over the casket was a large crucifix and to the left was a bronze bust of the Sacred Heart.

It was too solemn, the doctor thought. Jim, for all his religiousness, had never been a solemn man. He always had a smile and a joke, right up to the end. Indeed, the doctor remembered, the last time he had heard Jim say Mass, his brother had asked, "God's blessing on my brother and May and on those bastard Jesuits who are defying the Pope." They had been startled, but Jim had gone on serenely with the mass. Now his body was stiff and pale and his impish spirit was gone.

Doctor Collins had barely knelt down to say a prayer when he became aware that there were other people in the room. He said a quiet "Hail Mary" and "Our Father" and got up from the kneeler. He stepped to the left of the casket and looked at his watch. It was six-fifty. Calling hours were not supposed to start for ten minutes. Three women and a man had come in, and as soon as he got up, two of the women went to the kneeler. The doctor did not recognize them. He thought that perhaps they worked at the college. While the women were praying, an elderly couple entered. He did not recognize them, either. A moment

later, five people who looked to be in their twenties came
into the room, and he could hear more people out in the
lobby.

"I'm Father Jim's brother, Jack, and this is my wife,
May," Doctor Collins said, extending his hand to the
woman who was first to get up from the kneeler. "Thank
you for coming."

"Oh, Mr. Collins, we're so sorry to see Father Jim go.
He was a saint. We'll miss him."

"How did you know Father Jim?" May Collins asked.

"Everybody knows Father Jim," the woman answered.

As he looked over her shoulder, Doctor Collins could
see that the woman was not exaggerating. It looked as if
everybody was coming to the wake.

"My name is Doris. Are you the doctor?" the second
woman asked.

"That's right. I'm Father Jim's brother, the doctor."

"It's a pleasure to meet you, Doctor. I've heard your
brother talk of you."

"Then you were a friend of Jim's?"

"Of course. I loved Father Jim. He was the most
remarkable man I ever met."

"I'm glad to hear that. I always thought he was remarkable, too." The doctor's eyes scanned the room. "Seems
like he had a few friends we didn't know about."

"A few?" Doris exclaimed, and the two women
laughed.

One of the priests who had been on hand to greet the
Collinses stepped over to the doctor. "Have you seen
Father Rafferty?" he asked.

"Not since we arrived."

"He told me to tell you we're going to set up coffee out
in the lobby," the priest said.

"Did you expect all these people?" the doctor asked.

"No. And from what they tell me, this is just the beginning," the priest said and disappeared into the crowd.

Father Rafferty was sitting in a corner next to Cheryl. "Do you know all of these people?" he asked her.

"I know a lot of them, but not all," she said. "Some of them are from out of state."

"Out of state? Really? Where?"

Cheryl could not restrain a smile. "Well, some are from Rhode Island, some are from Connecticut. I'm sure there are people here from New Hampshire."

"Are they all A.A. members?"

"Not all of them, but the ones I know are," she said.

Father Rafferty was growing more and more curious. "What do they do? What sort of jobs do they have?"

"Do you see that man over there in the dark suit and the glasses?"

Father Rafferty nodded.

"He's a lawyer. And the man behind him is a college professor. Those two coming through the door — that taller man in his late thirties and the short one — they're newspaper men."

"Are there a lot of those?"

"I suppose, but not all of them come to A.A.," Cheryl said.

"Look at this crowd," Father Rafferty said. "It's not seven-thirty yet, and there must be more than one hundred people here. I was planning to have the Mass in the chapel here in Loyola Hall, but now I'm not sure. I talked to Fred and he suggested that we have it in St. Joseph's Chapel. But that's a huge place. It can dwarf a small congregation."

"Father Fred's right. At least I think so," Cheryl said.

"We could fit a hundred or so in the Loyola chapel," Father Rafferty answered.

"That Mass is going to be jammed wherever you put it," Cheryl said. "There's a lot more than a hundred people here, and they're coming and going. Wait until tomorrow. If all the people who knew Father Jim hear that he has died, you won't be able to fit them in Fitton field," she said.

"Really?" Father Rafferty asked. He was bemused by the thought of having Jim's funeral on the football field.

By seven forty-five, the room with the casket and the lobby outside were mobbed. The hum of conversation was loud and steady, and it was pierced frequently by laughter. The Collinses could feel themselves being caught up in the almost festive atmosphere.

"You know," a man in a dark suit was saying, "Father Jim once told me that when he got to heaven it better be pretty good or he'd damn well want to know the reason why."

Doctor Collins nodded.

"And he said he expected to meet all his friends there."

"He did have a lot of friends," Doctor Collins said.

"He was such an incredible person. He touched a lot of lives. But you know that much better than I do," the man said.

In fact, however, the doctor did not know. This was all new to him.

"I'll be right back. I'm going to get a sip of coffee," Doctor Collins said.

He left his wife and son talking to the man in the suit and moved slowly through the crowd. As he squeezed into the lobby, he found himself behind a bearded man who held a styrofoam cup with coffee in it and who was talking earnestly to the woman next to him.

"I don't think they know who Father Jim was," the man said, waving his free hand in the direction of the casket.

"None of them. The family. The priests. They all think Father Jim was just a nice, harmless old man. They have no idea."

"I suppose that's the nature of A.A. — Anonymity is the spiritual foundation," the woman said.

"Yeah, but you'd think his own family would have some idea of how significant he was. I mean, look at the people. Can you imagine how many people would be here if they all knew? Probably most of us haven't heard he is dead yet. He touched I don't know how many lives, and it wasn't just in A.A. He helped people in the gutter, in nuthouses, all sorts of people. If ever there was a Christian, Father Jim was it. He lived the Sermon on the Mount. That was his life. I guess his family wasn't from around here, but you'd think the other priests would know."

As Doctor Collins moved through the lobby, he found an almost party-like atmosphere as though the people had gathered to celebrate rather than to mourn. Priests who had known Jim for many years mingled with his A.A. friends, and both groups seemed eager to swap stories about him.

"I loved to go to confession to Jim," an elderly Jesuit told Bobby. "He would always tell me how much God loved me."

"He was something special," Bobby said.

"Apparently we didn't realize how special," the priest replied.

"You mean the people here didn't know about Father Jim?" Bobby asked.

"Well we knew he went to A.A. meetings and that he took a lot of cabs. The monthly taxicab bill — well you could ask the rector about it — was always astronomical. Did you know that the Yellow Cab company sent flowers?"

Bobby laughed. "Is that right?"

"They sent a large wreath, and all the flowers in it are yellow."

A third man now entered the conversation. "Yeah, it's over in the far corner of the other room," he said. "My name's Daniel," he said, extending his hand to the priest.

"Tell me, gentlemen, is Father Fred held in the same esteem as Jim?"

Daniel was precise both in this dress and his speech, and he now took over the conversation, weighing each word and measuring each sentence.

"They are or were very different men, but they both command a great deal of respect." Daniel was professorial in his demeanor. "Father Fred is introspective — quiet — a thinker. Father Jim was just the opposite. He had a will-o'-the-wisp quality."

Bobby nodded. "That's it, Cal. You're right. You couldn't put your finger on it."

"Cal?" the priest asked as if puzzled.

"It's a nickname I got," Daniel said. "People used to call me 'Silent Cal' because I didn't talk very much. Some people who knew me when, still call me 'Cal' once in a while."

"Oh," the priest said, still somewhat mystified.

"A lot of people were put off by Father Jim when they first met him," Daniel continued. "He was different. He had that smile. Some people thought he was senile. It used to irritate me when I first met him. I suppose because I thought he had something that I could never get."

"When did you first meet him?" the priest asked.

"I was staying on the hill," Daniel replied.

"The hill? Here?"

Daniel laughed. "No. The other hill. The one with the state hospital on it. I bounced around a long time before I came to A.A. to stay. Jim used to put on meetings at the state hospital and I used to go to get free cigarettes and doughnuts. I go way back with Father Jim, and Father Fred, too."

"That's remarkable," the priest said. "Silent Cal? In the state hospital? It's really hard to believe."

Daniel shrugged. "You'd be surprised how unremarkable it is. There are all sorts of people here with all sorts of stories."

The priest surveyed the room as if wondering just what kind of people he was rubbing shoulders with.

"Anyway," Daniel said, "It took me quite a while to figure out what was behind that smile. It took me years in fact. And what was behind it was enthusiasm for life."

"Yeah," Bobby agreed. "He just loved being. I mean the man suffered like you wouldn't believe. But he took life like it was a marvelous gift, in spite of the pain. He loved it. I don't know anybody who loved life the way he did."

"And he loved other people. He delighted in them," Daniel said. "And he never judged."

"And he loved to give money away," Bobby said. "He just loved to hand people money — whether they had money or not. He just loved to give it out."

"That I can believe," Doctor Collins said slipping into the conversation. "Jim was forever sending people to me to be treated, and when I would ask him how much I should charge, he would say, 'Jack, do it for nothing.' So I'd do it for nothing."

Doctor Collins paused and looked around the packed lobby.

"I must say that I'm amazed by all this."

"You mean the crowd?" Daniel asked.

Doctor Collins nodded, but it was not just the size of the crowd, it was the people themselves. They were all so sure that his brother was a special human being, that he had been instrumental in changing so many lives. He thought back to all the wakes he had been to — his father's, his mother's, friends'. He had never been to one like this.

A few minutes later, the word was passed. Father Rafferty had decided that the Requiem Mass would be celebrated in the large campus chapel.

"This is no ordinary Jesuit funeral," Doctor Collins thought. He went back into the room where Jim was laid out, silently clutching a set of rosary beads, and he was filled with awe.

— ✧ —

It was quickly apparent that Father Rafferty had made the right decision. No one counted heads. They didn't have to. St. Joseph's Chapel was filled to overflowing, and by the way they were clothed, it was obvious that the people came from all walks of life. The altar, too, was filled — sixteen of Father Jim's fellow Jesuits had robed to con-celebrate the Mass.

Kathleen, looking worn and full of grief, sat in the first pew with the Collins family. Bobby, Jerome and Anthony sat in the next pew, their faces solemn and sad. Among the other members of the congregation there were some long faces and damp handkerchiefs, but the vast majority of the people present had come to celebrate Father Jim's victory and not to grieve over his loss.

Father Rafferty opened the Mass and then mounted the pulpit.

"I welcome you, especially you members of Father Jim's special anonymous fellowship to this solemn and yet glorious occasion. I will not deliver the homily today. That duty has fallen upon Father Jim's friend, Father Fred. But I want to mention that I have known and loved Father Jim for many years.

"He was a man of many facets. He insisted, for example, that there be fresh coffee twenty-four hours a day. And he was always ready to answer the call. Always ready to aid someone in trouble day or night. And when he answered that call, he usually went by cab."

The long, slow sound of laughter rumbled across the church.

"And we of the Jesuit Community here at Holy Cross would like to thank the Yellow Cab Company for the flowers which they sent."

Again there was laughter.

"I want you to know that Father Jim was special to us as he was to you, and that as you will miss him, we will miss him."

Father Rafferty was silent for just a moment, and then he opened a large book and said, "The first reading is from the Book of Wisdom:

'But the souls of the just are in the hand of God, and no torment shall touch them. They seemed in the view of the foolish to be dead; and their passing away was thought an affliction, and their going forth from us utter destruction. But they are in peace. For if before men, indeed, they be punished, yet is their hope full of immortality; chastised a little, they shall be greatly blessed because God tried them and found them worthy of himself.

'As gold in the furnace he proved them, and as sacrificial offerings he took them to himself. Those who trust in him shall understand truth, and the faithful shall abide in him with love, because grace and mercy are with his holy ones, and his care is with his elect.' "

There was a pregnant silence as the congregation digested the words which Father Rafferty had read.

Jerome sat next to his aunt repeating the phrase over and over: "Gold in the furnace. Gold in the furnace." It seemed so appropriate to Father Jim. Jerome could almost feel his presence, could almost see his smile beaming from above the altar.

The second reading was from Revelations, and Jerome who had been lost in his reverie, missed the first part of it.

"...and he shall be their God who is always with them. He shall wipe every tear from their eyes, and there shall be no more death or mourning, crying out or pain, for the former world has passed away. The One who sat on the throne said to me, 'See, I make all things new. I am the Alpha and the Omega, the Beginning and the End. To anyone who thirsts, I will give to drink without cost from the spring of life-giving water. He who wins the victory shall inherit these gifts; I will be his God and he shall be my son.' "

Kathleen leaned toward Jerome and nudged him.

"Drink without cost. Anyone who is thirsty," she said.

Surely the readings had not been chosen by accident.

When Father Rafferty had finished, Father Fred walked slowly to the pulpit. He looked drawn and preoccupied. For many of the people in the congregation, it was the first time they had seen him wearing vestments — and the vestments set him apart — they made him seem distant.

"A reading from the holy gospel according to John," Father Fred said.

"Glory to you, O Lord," the congregation answered.

Fred cleared his throat and then he began to read:

"Martha said to Jesus, 'Lord, if you had been here, my brother would never have died. Even now, I am sure that God will give you whatever you ask of him.'

'Your brother will rise again,' Jesus assured her.

'I know that he will rise again,' Martha replied, 'in the resurrection on the last day.'

Jesus told her, 'I am the resurrection and the life; whoever believes in me, though he should die, will come to life; and whoever is alive will never die. Do you believe this?'

'Yes, Lord,' she replied. 'I have come to believe that you are the Messiah, the Son of God: he who is to come into the world.'

"This is the Gospel of Our Lord Jesus Christ," Father Fred said, looking out over the congregation.

"Thanks be to God," they answered in unison and sat down.

He leaned forward in the pulpit and waited for the noise to subside. His head was erect and steady. There was no trace of the head-wagging that had bothered him for so long in A.A.

"He is gone and left us with a sense of grief, a sense of deep personal loss, a sense that we can no longer pick up the phone or go to a meeting and hear his voice or see his smile. And so we are diminished; we are just a bit lonelier as we continue on our way.

"Just as you and I must, Father Jim has gone to be judged by his creator. And we know that the Judge is gentle. Many years ago, the founder of the Jesuits, Ignatius Loyola, told the men who were his early companions, 'I would rather be judged by Jesus Christ than by my own mother.' Think of that. Think of the tender reception that our friend is receiving as he displays the pages of the book of his life to the Lord. The story of his life will show his love and devotion to many people — to his fellow priests, to the members of our fellowship, and to many, many others whom Father Jim served because to serve them is to serve Christ.

"When I think of Father Jim, I think of the story about Saint John the Evangelist which has come down to us through tradition. Saint John lived on the isle of Patmos, and each Sunday at Mass he would give a sermon, and each Sunday that sermon would be on love. 'My children,' he would say, 'you must love one another.' This went on for years and years, until finally one member of the parish got fed up. During the week, he bumped into Saint John on the street. 'Father,' he said, 'all you ever talk about is love. Love. Love. Love. When are you going talk about something else?' And Saint John answered him, 'My son, there is nothing else. Love is everything.'

"For Father Jim, love was everything. Everyone who knew him recognized that. He was an example to us all. I know that I never met anyone like him — and I know that in the days and weeks and years ahead, I will miss him.

"But even as we grieve, we cannot forget that Father Jim has achieved his goal. Saint Paul, as he was nearing the end of his life, wrote in one of his letters, 'I have run the great race, I have finished the course, I have kept the faith. And now the prize awaits me.' Father Jim has run the race, and he has finished the course. His stay with us has been a success because he has received the most important thing that any human being can receive — eternal life. That was why he became a Jesuit. That was what he lived his life for. And now he has that wonderful prize. He is united with Christ forever — and we are still working and still striving, and hoping that we too, like Father Jim, will be welcomed by Our Lord when our time comes."

After the Mass, Father Jim's casket was carried a few hundred feet from the chapel to the small Jesuit cemetery in the center of the campus, and as the large crowd stood in the bright June sunshine, Father Jim was buried near the founder of the college and a few feet away from a friend of his who had won the Medal of Honor during World War II.

After the rites at the grave, the Jesuits invited all of Father Jim's friends back to Loyola Hall for coffee and pastry. On the way there, Daniel worked his way though the crowd until he was walking next to Anthony. The two former inmates at the state hospital walked side by side in silence.

Finally Daniel said, "Anthony, tell me truthfully, do you think Father Jim was really a saint?"

Anthony kept walking for a moment, thinking, and then he stopped, and Daniel stopped next to him right in the middle of the flowing throng.

"I'll tell you, Cal," Anthony replied, reverting to Daniel's old nickname, "if he wasn't a saint, he'll sure do until the real thing comes along."

Epilogue

The "jigginess" has long since left my brain, but even twelve years later, I still look back at that meeting — the last one that Father Jim ever spoke at — as a watershed. It was there that the seed of my recovery took root. It was there that an inner truth was revealed to me, and it was then that I began a new life.

And I still go, occasionally, to the small cemetery in the center of the Holy Cross campus and visit Father Jim's grave. When I go, I am almost unnoticed by the throngs of students or the handful of Jesuits who still live and work at the college. After all, it is my school. I am just another alumnus trodding the grounds, returning to say a quick prayer at the grave of a teacher.

Almost invariably, the memory of one night comes back to me. It was the night that I now know I first saw Father Jim. I was a senior and a few of us had gone off campus and bought a case of beer. We indulged in the time-honored sport of Dead Jebby Hurdling. One by one we raced the length of the graveyard hurdling the grave-stones of departed Jesuits — over and over, until the beer ran out.

As we left, we ran down the steps past him. He was thin and frail, hunched over and leaning heavily on his cane. In the moonlight, I saw his face — startled at first, then angry, and then as I scooted by him, it changed and I saw that huge grin appear. But in the moonlight, it looked ethereal, almost ghostly.

And I remember yelling out a wisecrack, "Was that a live Jebby or a dead Jebby?"

The morning after, as I tried to shower away the effects of the beer, I remember feeling guilty about that frail old man, imagining my words to have been cruel and cutting, as to most people they would have been.

But now, after all these years, I have the answer to my question. He was no dead Jebby. He was touched by life in a special way. It resided in him and it shone out of him. And I doubt very much if my intended sarcasm could have wounded him.

It is one of those paradoxes he was fond of. He lost himself, and yet he possessed more of life than anyone else I have known.

And it is another paradox that his life beckons to me. It calls me to follow his example, to be free from the bur-den of self — something I long for, something I fear.